LAW AND PEOPLE IN COLONIAL AMERICA

– BY –

Peter Charles Hoffer

The Johns Hopkins University Press

Baltimore and London

The Johns Hopkins University Press
701 West 40th Street
Baltimore, Maryland 21211–2190
The Johns Hopkins Press Ltd., London

The paper used in this book meets the minimum requirements
of the American National Standard for Information Sciences—Permanence of Paper
for Printed Library Materials, ANSI Z39.48–1984.

Library of Congress Cataloging-in-Publication Data

Hoffer, Peter Charles, 1944–
Law and people in colonial America / Peter Charles Hoffer.
p.   cm.
Includes bibliographical references and index.
ISBN 0-8018-4306-5 (alk. paper).—ISBN 0-8018-4307-3 (pbk. : alk. paper)
1. Law—United States—History.   2. United States—History—Colonial period,
ca. 1600–1775.   I. Title
KF361.H63   1992
349.73—dc20
[347.3]   91-26090

For Louis Micah Gareth Hull Hoffer

CONTENTS

N ear the end of Rodgers and Hammerstein's delightful *The King and I*, the king of Siam encounters a problem. Traditionally the giver of law, he no longer knew which laws were best for his people. He regarded himself as their father and wanted to do what was right for them, but his world and theirs was changing rapidly—too rapidly for him to understand the changes. Siam was becoming more modern, and his people sensed that the old ways were not necessarily the best ways. "Is a puzzlement," he concluded.

The king did not have a court historian, someone who could tell him how earlier kings had faced similar crises by adapting old laws to new situations. In plain fact, there is no way to solve the "puzzlement" of making good law without taking history into account. Today law plays a highly visible role in our everyday life. The courts are besieged with suits. Politicians and judges daily make claims and counterclaims about reform of our laws. The study of legal history has become a vital part of every American citizen's basic education.

We need to know about the history of our legal system in order to understand it because our legal system is inherently historical. American law requires legislators, lawyers, and judges to search the past for precedent. Every case brought to court has its own history, a "fact pattern," sometimes stretching back generations. Every case fits into a category of law whose origins may be centuries old. Every statute passed by the legislature has a history that the courts take into account. In the Anglo-American legal system, law is a dialogue between past and present, a continuing enterprise of interpreting the meaning of precedent and legislation.

Law and People in Early America

Law went everywhere in our early history. The first colonial governments were based on legal documents—"charters" and "letters patent." Colonial economies functioned under laws regulating prices, wages, and the quality of articles. Law gave the means for people to sell or will their land to others, provided a forum for settling arguments about broken fences and straying livestock, and even told people how to worship, marry, rear their children, and treat their servants and neighbors.

Throughout their colonial and revolutionary experience, Americans developed a passion for law, a legalism that pervaded social, economic, and political relationships. They laid their disputes with one another before the courts of law to an extent exceeding all other peoples. The colonists believed in the possibilities of a lawful world, and their demands for legal redress grew from and sustained this faith. Much that was American in our first laws and courts was driven by the needs and wants of the users of law; change in early American law came both from the top of society and from its middle parts.

In times of crisis, the intimate relationship between the forms of law and the aspirations of the colonists gained a transforming power. In the midst of the last of these crises, revolutionary lawyers labored to explain how rebellion was lawful and then set about reestablishing the rule of law. Legislators beset with the burdens of fighting a war for independence paused to argue about the shape of their new republic and wrote constitutions that substantially have survived to this day.

Two Controversies among Historians of Early American Law

Early American legal historians work in remarkable harmony with one another compared with scholars in some fields of American history, but there are two controversies among us about method that cannot be ignored. Both controversies concern how we explain change in law. First, some scholars regard the law as "autonomous" and largely self-contained, and believe that its language and practice act as a genetic code to control change. These historians focus on rules of law and "doctrines" that the lawyers, judges, and legislators formulate to explain law to one another. Alan Watson, a proponent of this "internalist" position, has argued that the key cause of change in law over time is the professional lawmakers' reading, or misreading, of the texts of manuals, cases, and statutes: "my often repeated argument that legal development—in the broadest sense of law: the structure of the system, its major divisions, the approach to the sources of law, and the legal rules themselves—owes a great deal to the legal tradition and, to a marked degree, is independent of social, political, and economic factors."[1] Often read in circumstances wholly unanticipated by their originators, these legal texts supposedly take on meanings that are neither useful nor reflective of the purposes of the drafters of the text.

Among the sources of "book law" available to the makers of American law, foremost were the decisions of the high-court judges of England—"precedent." These decisions were authority for all subsequent cases raising the same legal issues. Precedent was recorded in "reports" of cases, boiled down to its essentials in "abridgments" of case law by prominent scholars and judges, and explained in "treatises." In addition to case law, the statutes of Parliament were authoritative sources of law. Although the "rolls" of Parliament were locked away in the Tower of London during the era of colonization and no one was permitted to publish the debates in Parliament, the statutes passed by Parliament and agreed to by the king were published and distributed. Precedent and statutes together constituted the sources of law in England and its dominions, including the colonies. The colonists were proud to possess the common law but quick to question particular parliamentary statutes they thought unfair to Americans.

Unfortunately, one cannot assume that this rich body of book law accurately reflects colonial legal activity, because for the first one hundred years of colonial life, most American lawmakers had a very imperfect knowledge of English law. Few had studied it, and fewer still remembered all they had learned. Colonial legislators and lawyers recalled the general outlines of English law; time and distance blurred the details. Seventeenth-century colonial assemblies actually set aside funds to purchase English law books so that some reference works would be available. By the middle of the eighteenth century, leading American lawyers had amassed libraries of law books; lawyers made their influence felt in the assemblies; and young colonists went to England to study law, but the legal history of the colonies was already a century and a half old. Scholars know more today about English law than the colonists did, and it would be a genuine mistake for the scholar to impose his or her knowledge upon the minds of colonial lawmakers.

An alternative approach to the study of change in law explains shifts in law through an examination of shifts in society. Roscoe Pound of Harvard Law School pioneered this approach in America at the beginning of the twentieth century. He called it "sociological jurisprudence." Lawrence Friedman, one of the most influential modern advocates of this approach, terms it "law and society" and focuses not on the letter of the law but on the entire "legal system." He bids his readers think about lawmaking and law enforcement as part of a broader pattern of social interaction. He admits that there is a boundary between law courts and other institutions—the marketplace, the family, the church, and the schools, for example—but believes it is permeable, allowing ideas, customs, and feelings to pass in both directions. Friedman collects evidence from social, economic, political, and religious sources as well as the texts of law books, statutes, and judges' opinions.

A second controversy over the way to explain change in law overlaps the dispute over evidence but has independent origins and consequences. This controversy concerns the human sources of change. Some scholars seek out the makers of law—the elite or the professionals at or near the top of society—to find the causes of change. The interests, ideas, and aims of these people are the subject of such historians' accounts. Historians who focus on legal elites may argue that the elites were channelers of the aspirations and shared morals of the people generally, a "consensus" view of lawmaking, or aver that the elites manipulated law to serve themselves and subjugate the common people, sometimes called a "hegemonic" view of legal history.

Other historians prefer to emphasize the way in which the demands of the consumers of law, people who sue one another or press legislators to make new law, influence change in our legal history. Some of these historians stress the way in which change in the law reflected the competition of different economic and social interest groups in the society as a whole. Other historians in this school stress the wavelike patterns of reform and reaction in popular response to law.

The Themes of This Book

The two controversies among scholars of early American legal history are beneficial to everyone working in this field because they force us to be more thoughtful in our selection of evidence and more forthcoming in our thematic emphases. The externalist, law-and-society position expresses itself in this book's first theme: the reformist impulse of early American law. The story began in England, in protests against the severity and bias of its criminal law and the feudal relics of its civil law, and crossed the Atlantic. From the first settlements in New England and Pennsylvania, the settlers insisted on a more humane and forgiving criminal law and a more egalitarian civil law. As the colonies matured, these reform impulses were contained but never wholly curbed. They burst forth in the revolutionary crisis of 1763–76.

This book has a second theme: the energy pulsating through the first American legal systems blurred distinctions between public and private law. Public law includes constitutions, rules for government officials (for example, terms of office), and prospective general allocations of resources (such as a statute setting the price of land or prohibiting labor unions). In general, public law is made by legislatures or executives, not by courts. Private law concerns "mine and yours"—disputes over rights, duties, and property among individuals. Private law is confined to the parties, backward looking, and determined in court. The modern theory behind this division of responsibility in making law and adjudicating lawsuits is that the legislature ought to serve the whole people, whereas courts should concern themselves with individuals and their quarrels.

Early American lawmakers did not advocate such a distinction. Private bills for individual relief were a major business of the legislature, and courts heard and determined major public disputes. Colonial charters and grants spelled out who would rule and who got what parcel of land. Only when the colonial courts were politicized by the revolutionary crisis, and leaders of the resistance sought a doctrine to insulate the colonial personal rights from parliamentary public authority, did revolutionary lawyers press for a distinction between public authority and private liberty.

I do not want to claim that these themes are the "singing reason" of early American law. Quite the contrary; they did not work themselves pure but were always accompanied by countervailing forces—forces that they themselves called up. Against the populist clamor for a more just and accessible law the first magistrates arrayed themselves, sure that God or king had ordained them to make law and dispense justice. Even as law and courts created from above were altered by demands from below, reforms farmers and laborers sought were eroded by the same groups' increasing reliance upon professional legal counsel and by the formalities the lawyers imposed upon the courts. The overlapping of public and private law characteristic of the earliest settlements was in time of revolutionary reform undone, and distinct private rights were shielded by distinct public law doctrines.

Two Cautions for the Reader

A first caution: the history of law and people in early America is a very broad subject. It covers almost two centuries and stretches across two continents. Each of the thirteen English colonies that would become the United States of America developed its own legal system. Until the last few years of their history, individual colonies had closer ties to the mother country than they did to one another. The scope and diversity of the subject matter of this book make generalization necessary at the same time as they render generalization hazardous. There are exceptions to almost every general statement made in this book, and there is no way to mention all of these exceptions.

A second caution: Americans adopted much of the legal language of England even when they deviated from English legal practices. The words of law themselves are a part of our subject matter, and the words, like all transmitters of culture, had a history of their own. A word like trespass not only meant a physical invasion of one person's property by another person but also called up a series of technical legal categories that originated in medieval England. There is no way to omit all of these words from a history of law and people and no way to convey, in any survey, the richness and complexity of such words' histories. As with generalizations about time and place, I have tried to balance precision and simplicity.

ACKNOWLEDGMENTS

I wish to thank the many friends and colleagues who have put aside their own work to help me with mine. John H. Baker, Paul Brand, Bradley Chapin, Martin Flaherty, N. E. H. Hull, Milton Klein, David Konig, and William E. Nelson read the manuscript at various stages of its development and tried to save me from error. Members of the New York University Law School Legal History Seminar and the Philadelphia Center for Early American History made valuable suggestions for revision. I am especially grateful to Cornelia Dayton, Francis Fox, Judith A. Gilbert, Eben Moglen, Alison Olson and Deborah Rosen for sharing unpublished work with me, and Richard Beeman, Richard Dunn, John Murrin, Nancy Rosenberg, and Michael Zuckerman for their finely honed criticisms. Abraham Eisenstadt took an early interest in the book and helped steer it to its proper audience. Maureen Gilgore-Hewitt eased its passage on that voyage. Stanley Katz provided timely and gentle suggestions. Robert Brugger insisted I bring the manuscript to the Johns Hopkins University Press, and he shepherded it into the fold. Grace Buonocore copy edited the manuscript twice, demonstrating saintlike patience as well as skill. Louis Hoffer's enthusiasm for the project never flagged; he knew his father would dedicate it to him.

Law and People in Colonial America

CHAPTER ONE

"That the Said Statutes, Lawes, and Ordinances

May Be as Neere as Conveniently May,

Agreeable to the Forme of the Lawes

and Pollicy of England"

In the sixteenth and seventeenth centuries, the people of Western Europe stirred restlessly. Pride, ambition, and dreams of easy living bid British adventurers look across the Atlantic Ocean with longing in their eyes. Competing with rivals from Spain, France, the Netherlands, Portugal, Sweden, and the rest of western Europe, the British ventured into the great ocean beyond the pillars of Hercules, a "New" World. Ship pilots, trusting to their compasses and their fat-bottomed caravels, left the coasts behind and soon were joined by barks and brigantines filled with black-robed Jesuits and plainly garbed Pilgrims. The cold winters of New England and the malarial lowlands of the Chesapeake would drive off one in six of the newcomers, but the rest stayed to build homes, plant crops, and end their days in America. Woodlands Indians beheld the arrival of the great boats filled with "men of iron," saw the Puritans unload their cattle and their church bells, and knew that the world would no longer be the same. They were right—as Bernard Bailyn has written, "the westward transatlantic movement of people is one of the greatest events in recorded history."[1]

Imagine, then, a cold, tired, apprehensive assemblage of men and women—perhaps they were Christian Pilgrims, perhaps soldiers, craftsmen, and servants—gathered at the shore of the Atlantic, peering into a densely wooded wilderness. Clutching blunderbusses and Bibles, some must have summoned up memories of the world they had left behind. In their new world—Virginia, New England, and the other settlements of British North America—they would labor to rebuild communities, settle disputes among themselves, and fashion governments. They needed and wanted order, but most of them had little notion of the formalities of English law. Farmers and laborers, professional soldiers and servants, mothers and wives, they had seen and heard law, but not read or studied it, even if they were literate. A very few knew more. Gentle-born and educated, they had learned law and practiced it, as counsel, judge, or in Parliament. They could recite for their neighbors bits and pieces of the "book law" of England, but bits and pieces were not enough. Nor were the king's lawyers' written instructions for the colonists. These "charters"—part law code, part administrative rules, part policy guide—failed as formal sources of law, though the charter colonies would survive and the immigrants and their children would begin to transform the charters into constitutions.

Visions of the Law

What images of the law could the voyagers to Boston and Jamestown have brought with them to the New World? A few of the first colonists had the opportunity to visit the great royal courts at Westminster Hall at the edge of the Thames River. Even for men of means and education unpracticed in law, these courts would have seemed a noisy, throbbing beehive. The hall was already very old in 1600, its mighty timbers and vaulted ceiling a symbol of royal power. Thronged with petitioners and pleaders, smoky, dank, clangorous, and bewildering to any but the initiated few, the courts of King's Bench, Common Pleas, and Chancery occupied the drafty great hall. There were partitions between the courts, but not walls. The judges sat on raised platforms, and the pleaders sometimes had to outshout one another to be heard.

Here civil suits commenced, a veritable flood of litigation over land titles and broken promises, inheritance and trespass, flowing toward the great hall from all the corners of the realm. Ornate, taffeta-trimmed robes conferred gravity and authority on the king's judges. Robes also kept the aging judges warm; there was no central heating in the building. Costume denoted rank, and rank symbolized power. So did the mysterious language of the lawyers and the judges as they conversed with the familiarity of insiders. Visitors to the central courts had already heard bits and pieces of the language of the law—in the contracts, wills, and deeds that penetrated the most distant corners of the realm—but the operation of the courts themselves must have presented a daunting sight.

In the English countryside ordinary people saw the law rather than read it. Few English farmers could read, but many watched the law in operation at one time or another in their lives. Local courts met in newly built courthouses and halls of old castles—familiar places to which commoners were summoned to pay fines, give evidence, pray for the aid of the justices, or file legal papers. Some sat as jurors. When the king's judges arrived to "deliver" the jails of suspected felons and preside over their trials, village and field for miles around emptied their folk into the county town to see the procession of the law. The assize judges had traveled from Westminster, often on horseback, sometimes by coach, with them a train of clerks, attorneys, and their pack animals. The roads were muddy in late winter and dusty in late summer, the two times of year when the judges made their "circuits" of England's counties. The "home" circuit was the shortest; it took two or three weeks to attend court in the five shires around London. The Oxford circuit was the longest—eight counties to visit in a month—but also the most remunerative. The judges lived on fees, not salaries. The sheriff of the county sent his men-at-arms to meet the judges at the county line and guide them through the hazards that plagued the traveler.

At the edge of the county town, the sheriff himself went out to meet the judges, followed by the justices of the peace for the county, men of means and standing, and another flock of lawyers. Trumpets sounded and the bells of the town church pealed. The entire entourage proceeded to the church where the minister preached a welcoming sermon. That night there was a feast, and the curious craned their necks to catch a glimpse of the festivities. The next morning the judges presided over the selection of grand and trial juries and charged the juries with their duties. For the next three days, four if the jails were crowded, the judges presided at criminal trials. Jurors sat through the day, hearing and disposing of case after case. Often they mitigated the severity of the "book law." Despite the efforts of juries and the many pardons given convicted felons, the judges often left behind them gibbets creaking under the weight of dying convicts. Those returned to prison to await further proceedings were only marginally luckier than those upon whom the death penalty was visited. Prison fever carried away many; the food was awful (unless one was wealthy enough to pay the jailer for special privileges); and prisoners sometimes brutalized each other.

The judges also heard civil suits sent back for trial in the county after initial pleadings were filed with the central courts in Westminster. At these trials great and small appeared in person or by counsel to obtain redress. Often the judges directly queried the jurors to uncover their knowledge of the events and transactions in question.

Book Law

A handful of the American colonists exceeded their fellow immigrants in knowledge of the law. They had studied at the Inns of Court in London with other would-be barristers (literally those who sat "at the bar" in the Inns of Court) and were permitted to plead suits in the common-law central courts. These colonists not only saw the law, they had read it. The most important law on the books was the common law of England, in effect a language that pleaders and judges used in the king's courts. Source law included acts of Parliament assented to by the king and opinions of the king's judges. Common law could be found in "year books," student notes taken at the high courts as early as the thirteenth century. These stylized and terse compilations rarely recorded the outcome of the case, but they did give excerpts of judges' opinions and lawyers' arguments on complicated points of law. To this source, by the end of the sixteenth century, a few jurists had added their own commentaries. A student of law could also find a handful of treatises on special topics and "abridgments" of the common law.

In the era of colonization, jurists, judges, and magistrates produced a multitude of learned works. Foremost among this active generation of legal writers was Edward Coke, chief justice of England. His *Reports* of cases were then and are still regarded as the most informative of their day. Coke was a courtier as well as a judge, hardly a surprise in an era when judges were appointed by the king, often from among his political favorites, allies, and henchmen. As political as the process might be, the judges were also often very learned, and proud of it. What is more, the best of them truly believed that the king should not be above the law. Indeed, Coke was forced by King James I to step down from the bench in 1616, after an acrimonious and irreconcilable disagreement about who had the last word on the law. (Coke thought it should be the chief justice of England, but the king had other ideas.)

Undaunted by his demotion to private life, Coke began what would become his four-volume *Institutes of the Laws of England* (1628–44), the last volume of which was published after his death. The *Institutes* was unique in that it was written primarily in English and thus accessible to any learned man or woman, though Coke did discourse on Latin and "law French" texts and quoted long passages from them without translation. Coke, John Baker tells us, "delighted in wandering off at tangents."[2] Indeed, jurists like Coke were superbly well educated men; they loved knowledge for its own sake and displayed their erudition in the same way that other courtiers flaunted their clothes and jewelry.

Coke's and other contemporary collections, abridgments, reports of cases, and treatises were a hodgepodge of old and new, with the latest statutes alongside four-hundred year old judicial opinions. During his tenure on the bench, Coke tried to disguise his novel legal theories in the raiment of older precedent, and Francis Bacon, Coke's great rival on the bench, even essayed a complete codification of the laws; but in the end the great mass of the law remained unreformed and unpruned. The reason was simple. English law rested upon a doctrine of *stare decisis* (stand by decisions). Old judicial opinions were good law until they were overturned, and English judges did not like to undermine the very foundation of judicial authority. When necessary to depart from precedent, they preferred to distinguish the case in front of them from older cases, in the process of which they created a new precedent. Precedent was the fiber of which the common law was woven.

English Courts

Common law was not the only law in England. The king's courts had rivals. Saxon county courts predated the arrival of William of Normandy and his mercenaries in 1066, and county courts were not formally abolished until 1977 (though they had long before lost their major functions). The last Saxon king, Harold Godwinsson, lost his crown and his life to William of Normandy in 1066, and the Norman warriors who came with William not only imposed their will on the Saxons but also joined or replaced them as local judges. In courts of "baron and leet" held on the manor, the baron or his bailiff resolved disputes among tenants. In very attenuated form, manorial courts also survived into the twentieth century. Market fair courts and mayor's courts—some based on custom, others licensed by royal charter—regulated, among other subjects, transactions among merchants. The mayor's court of London was in many ways one of the most important courts in the realm.

The church held its own courts. They supervised the conduct of clerics, monks, and nuns, watched for heresy among lay people, oversaw the institution of marriage, heard disputes over bequests of personal property, and monitored sexual and moral conduct in the parishes. Before Henry VIII severed the tie between England and the Roman Catholic church, ecclesiastical courts were deeply involved in matters of state and sometimes ran afoul of the king's own courts. After the Reformation in

England, church courts were more obedient to the wishes of the crown, for the monarch had become the head of the church, but some decisions of church courts still had political repercussions.

County courts, manorial courts, merchants' courts, and church courts were all part of a pattern of concessions and bargains the kings of England made with their supporters and followers, but over time the king's own courts gained preeminence over their rivals. The king's "court" originally was the space around his person, a fortified zone guarded by his troops and his courtiers. The most important of these men advised him on legal as well as military matters. Out of the king's personal entourage, his council, the royal central courts coalesced. Legal reformers such as Henry II and, later, Edward I extended the reach of the king's law, affording civil litigants an alternative forum to which they could bring their suits. Increased business in the king's courts brought increased fees, always welcome to warrior-kings whose dynastic claims in Europe required the provisioning of armies for foreign war.

The busiest of the central courts were the Court of Common Pleas, which heard most civil suits; the Court of Exchequer, for royal financial matters; the Court of King's Bench, an appeals court with a limited original jurisdiction; and the Court of Chancery, which remedied injustices not covered in the other courts and unmasked corrupt officials. Over time, these courts replaced feudal obligations based on military allegiance and knightly service with common law and equity. The four high courts remained distinct from one another until the Judiciary Reform Acts of the 1870s brought them together. Other courts were created by the "prerogative" of the crown in the sixteenth century. Some of these, such as the Court of Star Chamber—a court "of inquisition" created by the Tudor monarchs to inquire into abuses of power— would, under the Stuarts, themselves become engines of tyranny. The greatest court was and remains Parliament itself, the king's great council. Originally called by him for advice in times of special need, Parliament remains a court to this day.

The king impressed his law upon the countryside by commissioning trustworthy members of his council and leading jurists to ride out from Westminster and hold court all over the realm. Henry II called these roving judges "justiciars," and they collected fees and brought back cases for his council. Under later kings, the periodic but irregular tours of royal commissioners were replaced by the biennial assize circuit courts. The king also commissioned powerful and respected men in each county to hold court as his justices of the peace. These justices not only acted as magistrates but also held court four times a year to enforce royal statutes, oversee the licensing of businesses, and keep the roads in good order. To these "quarter sessions" courts fell the onus of regulating morals taken from church courts after the Reformation. Serious crimes (crimes of "life and limb") were reserved to the circuit courts of assize.

The Justices of the Peace

The representatives of the system of royal justice that most colonists knew best (indeed, some colonists had held the office themselves) were the justices of the peace in the king's commission. In court and out they had the power to keep order, take and hold bonds for good behavior, and arrest and question criminal suspects. A judge, Anthony Fitzherbert, published a manual for justices in the early sixteenth century, and later volumes of this sort by Richard Crompton, William Lambarde (both local magistrates themselves), and Michael Dalton widely circulated in England and the colonies. Dalton's *The Countrey Justice* (1619) was the law book most often imported into the first English North American colonies.

The Countrey Justice was organized alphabetically, a handbook suitable for a man of affairs named to the county bench. On such "squires" the crown relied to control local troublemakers. Dalton's section on "peace" admitted that, in another context, the word might connote "amity, confidence and quiet that is between men," but that the magistrate should not concern himself with "uniting of minds." Instead, the justices were to suppress "any injurious force or violence moved against the person of another, his goods, landes, or other possessions, whether it be by threatening words, or by serious gesture of force of the bodie, or any other force used *in terrorem populi*."[3] The common law provided civil remedies for assault, battery, and trespass with force of arms, but the justice of the peace was a criminal magistrate first and foremost. He used his powers to establish a system to watch and warn against crime, binding suspects and potential disturbers of the peace by bonds and sureties put up by the defendant and by others, the latter often important men in the community. The recognizance bonds and sureties stiffened official justice with a network of unofficial, private restraints against misbehavior ultimately founded upon the economic and social influence of leading persons in the community.

As the king's justices in the era of colonization knew, the countryside was filled with unrest, with reason. Over a course of centuries, the poor had claimed and gained access to "common" land, including the forests and wasteland once used by the kings of England to hunt deer. Enclosure and commercial development of these lands by the king or his designees was a terrible blow to the poor cottagers. Lands once available to them for food crops and grazing of livestock were increasingly leased out to cronies of the crown, who hired "agents" to drive out the cottagers. The deforestation of the king's forests to build newly fashionable oak-faceted houses, when wood was the heating fuel for the poor of England, added to the burden of the poor, particularly in these years of very cold winters. The result was the debasement of the cottagers, who were driven off their land and made into wandering laborers. Ironically, fear of a flood of the wandering poor coursing down country roads and flowing toward Westminster caused the crown and its advisers much anxiety.

In the era of North American colonization, the danger of starvation became real. From 1586 through the 1640s there were a series of crop failures caused by cold weather. The prices of rye, peas, and other subsistence crops of the English poor skyrocketed. Worse still, the cloth trade, which employed many of the poor, lost ground to European competitors. In the east and southwest of England the poor began to starve. With the support of the crown and the Privy Council, magistrates were authorized to help the poor find food that wealthy "engrossers" (hoarders or merchants buying up grain for reshipment to the Continent) had stored away. The food was then brought to market and sold at minimum prices to the poor, or in some cases actually brought to the homes of the poor.

If local justices and the central government were sympathetic toward the starving poor, the relief offered to the poor was inadequate. The Poor Law of 1576 and later laws on vagabonds and the strolling poor had presumed that poverty was a moral problem. Local magistrates understood the underlying economic conditions that could turn the day laborer and the hungry weaver into rioters, but local authorities could not convince the crown that the problems were systemic. Instead, the crown viewed each crisis as a separate and discrete event. The "books of orders" that authorized justices to sell excess grain below market prices saved many poor people from death, but there was no overarching program to deal with unemployment in England until the twentieth century.

In this atmosphere of crisis, social protest was inevitable. When the relief system broke down, the poor turned to self-help—helping themselves to the grains hoarded by grain merchants. These largely spontaneous outbursts were led by unemployed cloth makers, artisans, and cottagers living on the margin of subsistence and driven over the edge when they could not find employment. When men led the rioting, the local magistrates took stern measures against them. When women led the mobs, the magistrates treated the rioters differently. One such "grain riot," in Maldon, Essex, demonstrates how the justices managed the interplay between formal law and local customs of protest. Told of grain merchants' ships waiting for loads of rye that might feed their own families and disgusted with the central government's inability or unwillingness to ban the export of grains (for the king's own advisers stood to make great profits from such shipments in spite of the laws against them), the women of Maldon and the nearby towns took their children in hand, marched to the ships, forced their way on board, and required the sailors to fill frayed aprons and bonnets with rye. The justices of the peace were not surprised by these demonstrations of local unrest. Justice of the Peace for the County of Suffolk John Winthrop reviled the "unrewliness of the poorer sort" who poached from the king's game preserves, broke into buildings, and pilfered food.[4]

To the Essex justices' requests to the Privy Council for assistance, the crown returned admonitions to keep order. Prudently, the justices decided to interpret their commissions of peace to allow lenient treatment of the demonstrators. The justices had at hand more disorder than they could possibly quell, and the local constabulary was itself often disorderly and unreliable. The justices' decision in Maldon was not an abdication of responsibility so much as a reasonable exercise of the discretion inherent in their authority. According to William Lambarde's manual, justices were expected to exercise a sound discretion in keeping the peace, admitting suspects to bond, hearing evidence on local disputes, and ordering compliance with the myriad of regulatory ordinances passed each year by Parliament. They had no professional police force on which to rely, only the aid of a handful of part-time bailiffs and constables. They exercised authority in part because they were already local magnates, important employers in their own right of local men and women, and representatives to the House of Commons as well as officers of courts.

The Maldon magistrates' first response, authorized by the "books of orders," was to buy the rest of the crop for distribution to the poor. After a delay of two weeks, warrants were issued for the ringleaders of the protest, and when these women were brought before the magistrates, they turned out to have been active in prior protests. A modernizing commercial economy, the "world system" into which England bought with its woolens and grains, preyed upon the poor in these communities, and poor women struck back with traditional forms of protest.

The official response to the bread riots typified the incremental and conservative tendencies of English law. The local justices of the peace knew that grain riots were part of a deeply rooted medieval custom of protest against innovation, in this case the increasingly burdensome activities of engrossers who bought up the grain and brokers who sold it to the Low Countries of the Netherlands and Belgium. As much as the common people of Maldon protested, however, England's merchants would not be denied. Despite the laborers' bread riots and, in later uprisings, threats against individual merchants, an emerging upper middle class led England into commerce and industry. The justices of the peace, one foot in a world of local custom, planted the other on the side of emerging capitalism. Although they might delay and waver, the justices crushed the protesters in the end.

Charters for Companies and Proprietors

The increasing complexity of the overseas trade that impoverished the unemployed of Maldon provided capital for the exploration of the New World. In the same years that the poor futilely protested their plight, commercial ventures by companies of "merchant adventurers" made many able and ambitious families wealthy. The emerging commercial elite wisely made its peace with an anxious landed aristocracy and looked across the seas for profit. The crown assisted this impulse, chartering limited joint stock companies for trade in the Baltic, the East Indies, and finally the New World.

The English were very late into this game; the Portuguese, Spanish, French, and Dutch had made landfall on the west coast of the Atlantic before any real effort was under way in England. The first English thrust, Italian merchant mariner John Cabot's brief voyage under the patronage of Henry VII, was not exploited until nearly a century later. A group of West Country men led by Walter Raleigh, Humphrey Gilbert, and their kin combined plunder of Spanish treasure ships with voyages of exploration under licenses from Queen Elizabeth. The West Country men not only charted the coast of North America and the Caribbean Islands, they also began to leave small outposts behind. Fishing fleets on the outer banks of Newfoundland, small settlements in what John Smith would later call "New England," and abortive fortresses on the coasts of Virginia and the Carolinas marked these first ventures. There was no turning back.

In the sea chest of every "sea dog" like Humphrey Gilbert was a royal charter empowering the settlement of new lands. To him and his heirs, if he should survive and succeed (although he died at sea in point of fact), Elizabeth promised "all the soyle of all such lands, countries, and territories so to be discovered or possessed as aforesaid, and of all Cities, Castles, Townes, and Villages, and palaces in the same."⁵ There were no castles or palaces where Gilbert was going; Elizabeth's legal draftsmen were thinking of Mexico and its treasures—but then, so was Gilbert. Nevertheless, there were riches in colonization, as England's predecessors in the exploration and conquest of the Americas had proved. If gold and silver could not be extracted, England's first expectation, there was trade to be consummated, forests to be stripped, and staple crops to be grown, harvested, and sold through English middlemen. Furs and tobacco were cash crops, the former obtained through the assistance of the Indians, the latter through the dispossession of the Indians. Agreements between the crown and companies of merchants, individual explorers, and proprietors granted land as payment for political or military service to the crown, illustrating the law's newfound amenability to commercial entrepreneurship.

The crown's response to the commercial allure of empire was to grant charters with legal conditions that were already antiquated in England while brokering a series of deals with eager companies of merchant adventurers to exploit the economic possibilities of colonization. The charters that the crown gave to private individuals or groups combined the old and the new. King James I, a proponent of the divine right theory of monarchy, told Parliament in 1610 that through his holy mandate he alone was responsible for ruling the colonial plantations and trading posts and for "my part, I thank god, I have ever given good proof that . . . never king was in all his time more careful to have his laws duly observed, and himself to govern thereafter, than I."⁶ He relied on his personal authority—not common law or parliamentary statute—to grant letters patent to the Virginia Companies of London and Plymouth. After all, the New World—or whatever part of it he could keep free of French, Dutch, Swedish, Portuguese, and Spanish rivals—was his to bestow.

The charter for the Virginia Company of London of 1606 thus combined remnants of feudal vassalage and harbingers of nascent capitalism. The former resonated in the language of "homage." The feudal knight was his lord's "man"; the entire feudal world was such a hierarchy stretching from the lowliest peasant through the nobility of the sword up to God. The king could rely on the assistance of his men in time of war; in turn, he rewarded them with the use of land. The bundle of possessory rights that each of these men had in the land could be quite complex under feudal conditions. "Fee simple" amounted to ownership, with the ability to sell and will the land away. Leasehold and copyhold were more limited bundles of rights to the land. At the bottom of the hierarchy, the "villein" held the land, in theory, at his lord's pleasure, though in fact the villein was not without rights. Relics of this feudal system abounded in the language of the Virginia charter. Land was granted to proprietors of the New World colonies in free and common socage as of the manor of East Greenwich, a reminder that the king would exact no rents or duties from the grantee but expected the recipient to defend the grant against the enemies of the king as feudal grantees had once defended the English border against raiders. The crown could always rescind the grant; in medieval England loyalty had been a treasured commodity. In fact, Charles I would take back the Virginia Company charter in 1624, and James II dissolved the Massachusetts Bay Colony charter sixty years later.

Another set of symbols of medieval sovereignty appeared in the charters. Medieval Christian kings could conquer and grant lands held by pagans or infidels because Christians were defenders of the true faith, according to the doctrine of "Christian conquest" that dated from the Crusades. "Holy war" among the armies of Protestant and Roman Catholic princes would devastate Germany between 1618 and 1648. Such wars were "conceived by the warriors as a struggle between a 'justified' or saintly army engaged in acts of piety against a demonic and damned enemy committing sacrilege."[7] Elizabeth's and James I's lawyers adapted this doctrine to empower the freebooting of the Drakes and Gilberts who served the cause of English empire. Indians' rights were extinguished: "Indians could be dispossessed of the land they claimed [and inhabited] by a race of cultivators destined by Providence to plant the seeds of a superior civilization in the New World."[8]

Elements of the language of the charter also were drawn from medieval borough franchises that the crown granted to individuals and groups, another quid pro quo whereby the crown gained taxes and manpower in return for a concession of limited self-government. Under charters, towns could hold their own councils. These grants of privilege were the legal precedent for colonial assemblies.

The entire system of medieval royal land grants for military service was antipathetic to commercial development. Indeed, the commercial revolution begun by the Crusades and spirited onward by banks and mercantile companies undermined the value of land held under feudal grants. Commerce inflated money and diminished the value of long-term rents and in-kind payments, the mechanisms by which the nobility supported their households. The rise of common-law actions to determine title to land and to enforce promises had already overthrown much of the legal foundation of feudalism. The Tudors tried to revive feudal obligations because they were a source of revenue but simultaneously grasped at the revenue-raising potential of colonization by laying a structure of commercial compacts on top of the older feudal relationship. The grantees were not only to guard the king's new frontier in America, they were also to share its wealth with the crown. Such new wealth, the Spanish had proved, could stiffen the sinews of a nation if siphoned into its treasury.

The theory of mercantilism—the term would come much later—required that wealth flow from the colonies into the mother country and that the mother country monitor and manage trade in both directions. Although the doctrines supporting mercantilism were not fully articulated in England until the second half of the seventeenth century, the English crown was aware of the favorable balance of trade in the Portuguese and Spanish empires. The fruits of empire had made these nations powers in Europe out of proportion to their natural resources and geographical size. Empire was to be encouraged. Thus, James I graciously granted to the first Virginians "all liberties, franchises, and immunities, within any of our other dominions, to all intents and purposes, as if they had been abiding and born, within this our realm of England, or any other of our said dominions."[9] These liberties were commercial as well as legal, or rather, the two were intertwined. The company and its representatives had license to trade and prevent any others, within or without the colony, from theft or plunder.

The charters also set a precedent for merging private and public law which would continue in the colonies long after the charters themselves had been superseded by other legal arrangements. The merchant companies were private ventures under English law. The charters reflected a private transaction between the king, acting in his person as the owner of all land in the New World, and the company board of directors. In effect, the charter was a form of contract. The king realized that the companies would send men and women to the New World, and he gave the directors of the companies the authority to govern their trading posts. The charters granted to merchant adventurers like Gilbert "full and meere power and authoritie to correct, punish, pardon, governe, and rule by their . . . good discretions." At the same time, the crown was aware that the colonies would not be purely private domains; they would be small polities. The drafters of the charter thus required that the laws the merchant adventurers made in their own settlements must be "neere as conveniently may [be] to the forme of the laws and policy of England." Even more vital, the crown lawyers reminded the merchant adventurers that they and their men were to act as true servants of the crown. In return for their allegiance they secured "all the privileges of free denizens and persons native of England." The vagueness of the language of these contracts, made even more indistinct by the distance and difference between the center of empire in Westminster and the wooded vastness of Virginia and New England, permitted the colonists to exercise a degree of self-government not encompassed in the wording of the charter. Written to abet the endeavors of a private corporation, the charters became the first expression of public law in the colonies.

The Irony of Transmission

The crown tried to use legal forms to give shape to a vast and uncertain imperial enterprise. The forms chosen turned out to be wholly inappropriate to colonization of the Americas, with unintended and unforeseen results. The colonies of Virginia and Massachusetts not only failed to fulfill the precepts of their charters but also bore no relation to merchant company trading posts. Both became commonwealths—self-conscious conglomerations of communities—instead of outposts of English capitalism.

At the heart of the irony was a legal question: what status had colonies in English law? In theory, they were part of the king's personal domain, but fact preempted theory. Far from England, thinly populated, rich in natural resources, and occupied by men and women who knew their own minds and grasped a bargain when they saw it, the colonies edged toward self-government. When English authorities tried to make the imperial system more efficient and responsive to the wishes of the crown, colonial elites cited their old liberties and dug in their feet. The pattern appeared early in Virginia's history and persisted until the final crisis, in 1776.

VIRGINIA

Although royal grants and patents to colonial proprietors persisted well into the eighteenth century, the Virginia Company of London, a joint stock company formed to exploit Raleigh's discoveries, went bankrupt less than twenty years after its creation. Despite the aspirations of the directors of the company and the generosity of its underwriters and stockholders, the little settlement at Jamestown foundered. Accustomed to the episodic work rhythms of England, short on agricultural laborers and long on gentlemen soldiers, and stuck in the middle of a fetid swamp at the confluence of fresh and salt water, the company's men weakened and died at a frightening rate.

Captain John Smith, a lively and well-traveled mercenary soldier who had signed on for the trip at the last moment, seized control of the settlement and refashioned it along military lines. He extorted from the Powhatan confederation of Indians what the Indians would not give or trade. Smith was recalled to England to answer complaints from his disgruntled comrades, but his methods were given legal sanction after his departure by "Dale's Laws." Sir Thomas Dale, named governor of Virginia in 1609 but shipwrecked on Bermuda for the first years of his tenure, administered "Lawes Divine, Moral, and Martiall" (for all the pitiless brutality of the code, it might have been titled the "Lawes Capitall") to institute order and save the colony for the company.

Dale's harsh code was modeled on the martial law in force in England's territories in Ireland and reflected the incessant warfare among the great European powers. Even when Europe itself enjoyed a respite from war, there never was peace among the Europeans in the New World. The first governors of the English possessions in the West Indies and on the North American mainland were "governors-general," professional soldiers with combat experience in Europe serving as the king's strong right arm in his far-flung domains. As Stephen Webb recently reminded us, "'governors'—the English title is of Tudor coinage—commanded garrisons in the capitals of the conquered provinces. Their troops marched out from urban citadels to enforce the orders the governor received from the crown and to collect the taxes he levied to support royal government."[10] There was little place for the common law in these military outposts.

While the agents of the company struggled to survive in their fortified enclaves, the directors exploited the powers of government and lawmaking given them in their charters. Eager to realize a profit from their investment and not fully trusting the integrity of the young men whom they had sent to Virginia, the directors kept the settlers on a very tight leash. They gave to their governors vast and untrammeled lawmaking powers, maintained the martial cast of the law, and rewarded particular planters with special concessions. For their part, the governors acted like soldier-lords, brooking no opposition from disgruntled settlers. By 1619, the long reach of the company and the absolutism of its governors were failing, and the leading settlers decided to take matters into their own hands.

Spreading across the face of the land, moving up river and across swamps, Virginia planters refashioned the legal system to their convenience. On their own authority (the company was too busy to notice; money was spurting from its coffers like blood from a ruptured artery, and the directors were trying to staunch the flow by running lotteries all over the south of England), Virginians created a representative

"House of Burgesses" to make laws. The House of Burgesses continued its work throughout the colonial period, becoming a model for subsequent colonial assemblies.

When word reached London that the planters had gathered in their own little parliament, Sir Edwin Sandys, director of the company in London, sought legal advice. He wanted to keep the planters happy, but there was no provision for a local assembly in the charter of the company. In his circle of acquaintances was the notable antiquary and lawyer John Selden, and Sandys asked Selden whether the laws of England or the rights of the crown prohibited a House of Burgesses. Sandys wanted Selden to examine all the charters and justify the colonists' initiative. Selden, able counsel that he was, found grounds for a local assembly along the lines of a town council in the words of the original letters patent of 1606. Put in more familiar terms, Sandys was seeking to link English law to colonial law, now that there was a lawmaking body in the colony itself.

MASSACHUSETTS

As the planters and servants of the staple-crop colonies of Virginia were settling down to the cycles of planting tobacco, girding themselves against the Indians, and making laws, the ailing Virginia Company of Plymouth was selling its right to occupy New England to another group of men, much different in cast from those in Virginia. Soon, whole families—indeed, entire villages led by their magistrates and their ministers—would embark for New England. Some brought with them a fear of religious persecution. A small band of "Pilgrims" had already left the northeast of England, sojourned in Leyden in the Low Countries, and settled themselves in Plymouth. They severed their ties with the English church and sought to create a simple biblical commune in the New World. A larger number of emigrants were "Puritans." Wealthier and more aggressive than the Pilgrims, the Puritans had labored at great prejudice to their own fortunes and safety to reform the English Protestant church. Many of them came to the New World to escape persecution at the hands of King James of England and his bishops. The king's "prerogative" courts, primarily the Court of Star Chamber, and the ecclesiastical courts, dominated by the king's appointees, made life and worship very difficult for the Puritans.

The courts were effective tools against Puritans in part because the Puritans themselves placed great value on law and legality. Some Puritans were members of Parliament and had pressed for statutes punishing sexual immorality, vagrancy, and other exhibitions of moral laxity. Some among their number studied law and became lawyers. They lobbied for simplification and rationalization of English law. Even the sermons of Puritan ministers had the flavor of lawyers' briefs. For these men and women, the Bible was a source of law as well as a book of devotion. Puritan ministers articulated a covenant theology comparing the Puritan's relationship to God to Abraham's pact with God. The gathering together of Puritan "saints" in New England thus rested upon a renewal of the covenant, a word with meaning in both law and Holy Scripture.

Before leading Puritans gathered their families and fled from persecution, they would purchase from the Virginia Company of Plymouth and take with them the official copy of the company charter. It rests now in a showcase in the Massachusetts Statehouse. The Puritans had to have the charter, a corporeal embodiment of law, to prove to themselves the lawfulness of their flight.

No sooner did the Puritans set foot on the Massachusetts shore than the leaders of the colony discovered how difficult it was to impose the covenant ideal of law upon all the settlers. Ashore, assembled under mighty oaks, they did "covenant with the Lord, and one with another and doe bynd ourselves in the presence of God to walk together in all his waies."[11] The contractarian beginnings of their new churches and towns transformed the old chartered trading company into a commonwealth, but the Puritans' alloy of legalism and piety never did prevent internal dissention. When a portion of the inhabitants of Salem Village ordained their new pastor, Samuel Parris, in 1689, they agreed "that we may keep this covenant, and all the branches of it, inviolable forever," but three years later the men who agreed to keep the covenant were accusing one another of harboring and abetting witches.[12]

As contentious as these New England communities might be, they were in fact remarkably law-abiding given the potential for disorder. The emigrants' commitment to law brought a political community out of scattered settlements on the edge of an ocean. Whether they believed themselves saved or damned, they agreed to divide the land, secure local order, regulate trade among themselves, and defend their towns against the crown. This required government and law. Indeed, their repression in England induced them to rethink the operation of law and gave impetus to what would become a far more thoroughgoing revision of law and courts than was ever attempted by Puritans in England.

The leading planters who had purchased the bankrupt Virginia Company of Plymouth transported it and themselves to the New World and transformed its board of directors into a ruling political council. These "Assistants" assumed supreme judicial authority. Led by newly elected Governor John Winthrop, the Assistants preferred to hear and determine lawsuits without a code of laws, but pressure from the deputies elected by the towns induced the Assistants to commission Nathaniel Ward, who had legal training, to draft a "Body of Liberties" in 1641. Ward's effort was the basis of the "Laws and Liberties" promulgated in 1648. The latter were adapted by the Puritans who formed the colony of Connecticut.

The Liberties promised Massachusetts men, and to a lesser extent women (for women were not full partners in the political or legal life of the colony), that they had rights and privileges. A written code of law also increased the security of property. The Liberties combined public and private law—government power and personal deportment were both fit subjects for the Massachusetts lawmakers. In language reminiscent of the "Great Charter" of English liberties (Magna Charta), the Liberties promised an even-handed law:

> No mans life shall be taken away, no mans honour or good name shall be stained, no mans person shall be arested, restrayned . . . no mans goods or estate shall be taken away from him . . . unlesse it be by vertue or equitie of some expresse law of the Country waranting the same, established by a general court and sufficiently published. . . . Every person within this jurisdiction, whether inhabitant or forreiner shall enjoy the same justice and law, that is general for the plantation.

At the same time as the Liberties affirmed "the same justice and law" for all, the inhabitants understood that legal rights were not abstract principles but were woven into the fabric of Puritan community life. Although Governor John Winthrop had opposed the drafting of a code, he need not have worried—the magistrates retained much of their discretion. Equal protection of the laws did not forbid special privileges— quite the contrary; gender, wealth, family, political position, and, above all, religious persuasion made a difference in one's legal status. The Puritan way of worship in congregational churches and Puritan religious doctrine, a stern version of Calvinism, were established by law in Massachusetts and Connecticut, and woe be to the Quaker or other sectarian who persistently flouted the will or questioned the privileges of these favored institutions. If property or liberty could not be taken without color of law, that is, only by a warrant or during a time of emergency, the "expresse law" was infinitely malleable. All adults had the right to make any "lawful" (a limitation inviting abuse of discretion by the government) address to the courts or the government, enter into contracts, be protected against frauds and duress, and leave the colony at will—unless, of course, the authorities wished to detain them. The Liberties established formal courts, superseding the Assistants' assumption of jurisdiction, though the Assistants were confirmed as the central court in the colony.

The system of civil pleas in the Liberties resembled that in the English local courts. No lawyers were invited or encouraged to practice, though lawyers evidently did bring their skills to the colony and earned a living writing legal documents. Juries were impaneled to decide questions of fact and give "special verdicts" if a point of law was disputed among them. Only the court, in open deliberation, could distrain property or detain persons. No torture was permitted, unless an already condemned felon was suspected of taking part in a conspiracy. This provision the Puritans borrowed from the English prerogative courts, ironic in light of the Puritans' dislike for inquisitorial methods.

There was also in the Liberties a list of what would today be called procedural rights. Public and speedy trial, the defendant's power to call witnesses, the right to testify under oath (a right not allowed felony defendants in England until the eighteenth century), and the right to a jury trial were all guaranteed. The code also granted the status of "freeman" of the towns to male members of the churches. Freemen could vote, hold office, and voice limited dissent. The subordinate status of women, servants, and children was also defined in the Liberties. The Puritans were never social egalitarians, and ministers and magistrates agreed that women and minors ought to be legally subordinated to free adult males. A list of crimes and punishments, in effect a penal code, followed the civil provisions, some of the former taken from English criminal law, others from the Old Testament.

The frequent recourse to the Bible in the Liberties was more than window dressing but less than an attempt to rebuild Jerusalem. In fact the code tracked English law, not the Old Testament. Nevertheless, the citations to the laws of Moses told a story of their own. Adultery and blasphemy, misdemeanors in the common law, were made capital crimes in Massachusetts, as were apostasy and disrespect to parents. Yet Massachusetts men and women were almost never prosecuted for these offenses, and even those few prosecuted very rarely suffered the prescribed penalty. In the one case of prosecution for abuse of parents, the parents themselves stepped in and pleaded for the life of their son.

The dockets of the criminal courts show that there were many cases of fornication, but only two married people were ever executed for committing adultery. Blasphemy was punished, but not by death.

The Puritans mitigated punishment for most of their Old Testament crimes because the laws were not meant to function in a literal way. The borrowing of Old Testament injunctions was a solemn public warning to those at the edges of the Puritan community against violation of the deeper social mores that held the Puritan towns in the wilderness together. The purpose of severity in the book law was as much to get the attention of potential wrongdoers as it was to punish actual wrongdoers. One consequence of the admonitory function of criminal law was that almost everyone presented to the magistrates for disorderly conduct or other minor offenses was chastised in some way. The criminal justice system did not function solely or even primarily to determine guilt or innocence, but to restate deeply held social values.

As the New Englanders dispersed themselves into town grants along the rivers and up and down the Atlantic coast, they named local magistrates to hear disputes among the acquisitive and quarrelsome. Though often styled "peaceable kingdoms," even the best behaved of these towns could erupt in contention. What was peaceable about them was their willingness to subordinate individual desires to duly appointed authorities, at least most of the time. When a faction or a family would not submit, it was invited to leave. The respected men and women of the town policed their neighbors, but some official was necessary to impose penalties on those who could not be persuaded to live peaceably. One of the earliest of these commissions for local justice survives. In the Connecticut River settlement of Agaam, or Agawam, later Springfield, on February 14, 1639, the inhabitants "did ordain" William Pynchon, who in fact had recruited most of them from England and employed most of them and their families, to "execute the office of magistrate."[13] He was to administer oaths, issue warrants, process executions (the return of the warrants), order attachments (of property to pay damages to the winner of a court suit), examine witnesses in misdemeanors and civil suits, inflict corporal punishment, imprison suspects until trial, impanel juries, hold court, and keep the court records. These powers were similar to those of the English justices of the peace but somewhat more expansive. New Englanders assumed that local authority was best placed in the hands of those with high economic and social status.

Like the stranger in biblical Jewish kingdoms, everyone in the Puritan commonwealth was to be judged by the same law, but the price of such formal equality was that non-Puritans, people with different

ways, values, and cultures, were not allowed to claim the protection of their own laws. Even though the Indians were the original inhabitants of the land, Puritans regarded Indian hunting grounds and
villages as uninhabited, "virgin" land because the Indians were not
proper cultivators. In fact, the Indians were able and successful cultivators. Their slash-and-burn agriculture allowed the planting of very
nutritious food crops—the corn and potatoes that, exported to the Old
World, would all but end famine in Europe. The clearing of under-
growth also permitted the native grasses to flourish, in turn feeding
browsing game such as deer. The first English settlers benefited from
Indian agriculture, though in time the English would replace browsing
grasses with clover and rye, and the deer would give way to cattle.

When it was not possible to ignore Indian cultivators' claims, New
Englanders "purchased" the land. Under the Liberties, Puritans trans-
ferred title to land through deeds. Both parties to the deed supposedly
knew what was happening, and the courts would protect the rights of
the party deceived by an artful buyer or seller. The deed gave to the
buyer or grantee full control of the land. Others stepping onto the land
without invitation were trespassers and could be prosecuted at law.
The Indians were invariably the losers in these transactions because
they had no conception of absolute possession of land. They thought
they ceded to the colonists the right to hunt and traverse the land—a
very limited right, which did not foreclose the Indians' own right to
hunt the land, set their traps on it, and gather fruit and plants—but
Puritan buyers claimed the whole bundle of possessory rights. Not all
the New England governments were unscrupulous in these dealings—
Rhode Island's policy was far more enlightened out of a mixture of
genuine concern for the Indians and fear of the colony's own weakness—but the legal systems for holding land in the two cultures were
irreparably dissimilar and in the Puritans' courts the Indians invariably lost out despite the "same justice."

In time of Indian war, the Liberties were silent. Slighted, shamed, or
angered, Indians raided, burned, and killed from ambush. The Puritans' response was vicious and conscienceless. In the Pequot War, indian villages were burned to the ground; women and children perished
with the warriors. Indians at peace with the Puritans, even tribes of
"praying Indians," were attacked by whites, forced to leave their villages, and confined in "safe" compounds. The magistrates and deputies
of Massachusetts Bay saw no parallel between their brethren's struggle
for autonomy in the English civil wars and the Indians' desire for self-
government in New England. At war the Puritans differed not at all
from their European counterparts. In the Thirty Years' War in Germany

(1618–48), no quarter was given noncombatants. Oliver Cromwell, leading a Puritan army to quell a rebellion in Ireland (1649–50), deliberately set an example to would-be Irish patriots by killing every woman and child in the rebellious towns of Wexford and Drogheda. Puritans in New England equalled these atrocities.

There was a final twist to the sad tale of the Puritans' legal relations with the Native Americans. The Puritans consistently maintained that the "title" to land they purchased from the Native Americans was valid. At the end of the century, a number of Puritans transplanted themselves from towns in New England to what would become Newark, in New Jersey. There, they purchased from native tribes "titles" to thousands of acres. Fifty years later, a group of well-financed land speculators challenged these land titles, claiming that the Native Americans had no right to land and thus could pass no title to the Puritans. Only land grants from the crown were legitimate. The descendants of the New England Puritans angrily replied that the Native Americans were never conquered by the sword and title derived from the native "owners" was valid. When the Puritans lost their case in court, they took to the streets in a display of the very sort of disorder that English and New England magistrates had so energetically quelled. The transplanted Puritans found themselves harassed and dispossessed, just as the Native Americans had been two generations before.

Sectional Differences in the Law

King Charles I of England knew that the course of development of the Massachusetts and Virginia colonies had proved the weakness of the charter system of transmission of law. He thought seriously about dispersing the colonists of Massachusetts and taking back the charter, but political troubles closer to home prevented him from acting. He welcomed Virginia as a royal colony but could not prevent Puritans from moving to it and trying to undermine his authority in it. He could and did use his power to reward his friends and punish his enemies in the colonies, but he was too far away to disturb the emerging patterns of colonial self-governance.

Meanwhile, Virginia and Massachusetts law responded to growing differences in the composition and internal development of the two colonies. Virginia soon became an entrepreneurial society whose need for labor, geographical expansion, and protocapitalist ethos developed cheek by jowl with the emergence of a successful planter elite. The Chesapeake colonies (Maryland soon joining Virginia) were restless, dynamic, fiercely competitive, and highly mobile societies, whereas the Puritan settlements, though interested in material improvement, were nonetheless more stable, close-knit, and communitarian.

Despite the early distinctive character of the two areas of settlement, it would be a mistake for the legal historian to divide the legal system of the colonies along a geographic line or between Puritan and Cavalier types of settlements. Puritans went everywhere in the colonies, bringing with them their keen instinct for the imperfections of the world and their brittle reaction to any dissent but their own. A visitor from Boston would understand the laws of early Virginia, and in fact Puritans soon made the trip, prayer books in hand and eyes on the abundance of land in the "Old Dominion." Nor were planters confined to the South; great farms in New England were markers of the entrepreneurial skill and "influence" of the "best" families. These northern planters used the law to promote their own interests. Although there were differences in use of space and life-style, lawmakers in both North and South had adopted much English local law, magisterial institutions, and regulatory inclinations.

At the same time, without fully realizing the implications of their actions and surely without intending all the effects of those actions, the colonizers of Virginia and Massachusetts were groping toward what would become an American way of law, a style of keeping order and resolving disputes which diverged in significant respects from the English. From the inception of the colonies, ordinary men and women had taken part in the making of law. Their laws and courts were more open and accessible than the myriad enclaves of special pleading and privilege in the mother country. The distinction in England between governance—the preserve of the king and his advisers (among whom technically were the members of Parliament)—and private law adjudication was all but lost in the easy passage of well-to-do colonists between their assemblies and their country homes.

The crown never intended that distinctive legal cultures emerge in the northern and southern colonies, any more than the crown wanted its chartered companies to become commonwealths in the wilderness. Viewed in this very narrow way, the transmission of English law to North America was a failure of vast proportions. It is important to remember, however, that the transmission of English law to the colonies did not stop with the foundation of Massachusetts and Virginia. As English law changed in the remainder of the seventeenth and throughout the eighteenth century, these changes too were transmitted to England's colonies. As we shall see, substantive law in the colonies actually moved closer to English common law as time progressed.

What is more, seen not as a purely legal matter but as a guide and helpmeet to the unparalleled movement of peoples from one continent to another, the transmission of English law was a success.

In what may be regarded as a final irony of transmission, the laws and courts in the first colonies of British North America began reforms still strongly resisted in the mother country. If by reform of law one means that more people can understand the law and have a hand in its creation, that the courts are more responsive to popular feelings and needs, and that the people respect the law, one must conclude that the first colonial legal systems had reformed some of the worst abuses of English laws and courts.

CHAPTER TWO

"And to the End that All Laws Prepared by

the Governour and Provincial Council Aforesaid,

May Yet Have the More Full Concurrence

of the Free-Men of the Province"

I n the first years of the seventeenth century, a growing stream of newcomers flooded the rocky coast of New England and rolled up upon the lowland shores of the Tidewater. Soon additional colonies of England dotted the Atlantic's western rim. As the colonial enterprise spread, the reception of English law and courts was shaped by local setting. The American forests, vast stands of hardwood and evergreen through which a person could walk for hours and not see another person, could not be mistaken for the fields and lanes of England. Instead of Norman stone churches in centuries-old villages, there were rough-hewn wooden churches in clearings. The majesty and mystery of the English law, its detail and its variety, could hardly be received unchanged in such a setting. Americans did not erect great halls of justice in the seventeenth century, nor endow Inns of Court, nor purchase extensive libraries of law books.

The American Difference

By the end of the seventeenth century, the American "court day" would have its own visual signposts. They would be more intimate in scale than those of England, but just as important a part of community life. The wood or brick courthouse would stand in the center of the county seat, its yard filled with jurors, lawyers, witnesses, and spectators when the quarter sessions court was in session or the supreme court arrived for its semi-annual visit. The pillory and whipping post would be erected nearby. A rude jailhouse would complete the scene, sometimes filled with men and women too poor to pay court costs that burdened the innocent as well as the guilty, or meaner sorts waiting for their trials in felony cases. Here the great and humble mingled, acting out the law in complex rituals of deference and dignity. As Rhys Isaac has written, "it would be hard to overemphasize the importance of the cermonial at the center of the coming together on court day."[1]

In the second wave of colonization, stretching from the 1630s to the end of the seventeenth century, the law was still imposed upon the settlements from without and above, but popular protest and shared hardship demolished feudal fantasies and undermined martial regimes. In the colonies of the seventeenth century, the codes and courts that emerged promised equal protection and representative government to those with property. If not the reform that Puritans envisioned, the first colonial legal systems did offer greater access to courts than the emigrants had known in the Old World. Thus, differences—the differences between English courts and American courts—were not a mere matter of detail; differences were signals of attitudes toward the function of courts in a society.

THE STRUCTURE OF THE COURTS

Unlike the English system of compartmentalized and specialized tribunals, almost all of the seventeenth-century colonies developed an overlapping hierarchy of courts. Petty sessions held by the justices of the peace were the lowest level of official tribunal. Above them sat county courts. Supreme or superior courts were the highest courts in the colony. The jurisdiction of the lower courts was limited by the jurisdiction of the higher courts. At the same time, a case might move from a lower court to a higher court on "appeal" and be reheard in its entirety—from initial pleading to jury verdict. In that sense, as Wilfred Ritz has written, our first courts were as much "horizontal" as they were hierarchical.[2] Often the same men sat as justices in local courts and judges on the high courts (as was occasionally true in England). Additional courts were created by legislative act (for example, probate courts to distribute property of those who died) or reappeared through the agency of the church (for example, vestry courts to discipline the impious and immoral).

In almost every colony, the county court was the workhorse of justice. Meeting as a court of "common pleas," it heard civil suits. Reconstituting itself as a court of "general sessions of the peace," it performed the regulatory tasks of the English quarter sessions courts and disposed of serious misdemeanors. The only limit on the jurisdiction of the county courts was that they could not hear cases of life and limb (felonies) or civil business in excess of some monetary ceiling. The justices of the peace who held court were drawn from the landed elite of the county and might be trained in the law. The first colonial county courts were often held in the houses of men of means, and some of the most important figures in the colonial government began their careers as justices of the peace.

County courts regularly heard the presentments of the grand juries, men of some substance and standing in the county. The offenses the grand jurors presented to the court tended to run in waves determined by changing regulatory statutes, the arrival or departure of certain disreputable individuals, and deeper alterations in social values. The justices also heard lawsuits among planters, yeoman, servants, and, on rare occasions, Indians. Most of their business concerned the survey, sale, and inheritance of land, but a significant portion revolved around personal status and dignity. Servants wanted better treatment from their masters; possession of slaves was contested; bouts of drinking led to assaults; families quarreled about wills.

Above the county courts were colonial courts of superior jurisdiction, sometimes styled supreme courts. In Massachusetts, this was the Court of Assistants, the governor's council wearing their judges' hats. After 1692, the judges of the court were appointed by the crown and went on circuit, meeting twice each year in the various county seats. The position was severed from the council, though many judges were also councillors. Holding more than one office was not barred in the colonies, and there were high-court judges who were also legislators and governors or lieutenant governors of their colonies. In Virginia, the General Court sat only in Williamsburg, the colonial capital. The judges of the General Court were the governor and his council, an arrangement that persisted until the outbreak of the Revolution.

DIVERSITY

A variety of distinct courts of limited jurisdiction in the colonies betrayed individual colonies' particular origins and interests. In the southern colonies, whose slave populations increased dramatically throughout the eighteenth century, special freeholders' courts of "oyer and terminer" for slaves were created along lines first suggested in Barbados. There were no juries in these courts; the freeholders—slave masters all—determined facts and meted out punishment. In South Carolina, all civil business was heard by the court of common pleas in Charleston, entailing a complex system of delivery and return of writs in the hinterland monitored by a "provost marshall." Maryland's proprietors, the Calverts, tried to force a legal system based on the Palatinate of Durham down their colonists' throats—with ill success. Later courts in the colony nevertheless showed great receptivity to English legal forms. In the colony of New Haven, the magistrates were more concerned with biblical injunctions than those issued by the English chancellors.

Alone among the New England colonies, Rhode Island made conciliatory gestures to England in the form of overt borrowing of English laws, but it is not clear that the references were anything more than advertisements for the loyalty of these colonists. In fact, Rhode Island courts were elective and communal, much like the rest of the governing apparatus of the colony. The text of the "Agreement" among the founders of the colony, transcribed and preserved by Roger Williams, shows that Rhode Islanders reserved for themselves the right to make their own laws: "We doe voluntarily assent, and are freely willing, to receive, and to be governed by the Lawes of England, together with the way of the administration of them, so farr as the nature, and constitution, of this plantation [colony] will admitte. . . . [but] We desire to have full power, and authoritye, to transact all our home affaires, to trye all manner of causes, or casses [cases] and to execute, all manner of executions [that is, to carry out all orders of their courts] as the collonye shall be pleased to refer, to generall tryals and executions."[3] The delegates also insisted on the right to appeal from town courts to the colonial General Court and the right of the citizens of the towns to choose all the town officers. The Rhode Islanders were understandably nervous about their claims to the land—they had no charter until Roger Williams went to England and secured royal assent—and did not want to offend English authorities. At the same time, there is much independent spirit in this 1647 Agreement.

Before 1700, courts in the "middle colonies" of New York, Pennsylvania, and New Jersey also evidenced those jurisdictions' particular beginnings. Their courts differed from both English and other American structures. After 1700, these differences began to disappear, though remnants of them would survive well into the nineteenth century. When the Dutch West Indies Company founded its colony in New Netherland, the directors intended to maintain a trading post with the Indians. The Indians traded furs, the latest craze in European haberdashery, to the Dutch, in return for tools, trinkets, and "wampum," strings of shells that the Indians used as a medium of currency. In effect, the Dutch introduced the Indians to a market economy and transformed Indians' relations with one another. New Amsterdam was a fortified town, "Wall Street" just that, a wall across lower Manhattan, but the settlers did not obey the instructions of the directors of the company. They wanted a form of self-government and to that end insisted on charters for their towns. A series of weak and dissolute governors, aided and abetted by a crew of inept and often inebriated legal advisers, conceded much to the burghers of New Amsterdam, but the last governor, Peter Stuyvesant, bullied the townspeople into obedience. The internal struggle for legal authority only ended when the Duke of York's English fleet arrived and the Dutch surrendered their colony to the English.

Disputes among merchants in New Amsterdam and the Dutch towns up the Hudson River were heard in the burgomaster's (mayor's) courts. These courts used Dutch law, which in turn was a variety of Roman law going back to the compilations of the emperor Justinian in the sixth century of the Modern Era. When the English conquered the Dutch in New York during the Anglo-Dutch War of 1664, the victors made the sensible decision that a few Englishmen could not dominate a hostile population of Dutch settlers. Instead, newly installed Governor Richard Nicolls agreed to keep the Dutch courts open if the Dutch would swear allegiance to the English crown. The Dutch agreed. The "Duke's Laws" of 1665 in the colony also established courts of sessions similar to the New England county courts for Westchester and Long Island, where many Puritans had established towns. Finally, to the Dutch and English grandees who held extensive farms on both sides of the Hudson River, the governor granted the right to hold manorial courts, recalling the privileges Norman magnates gave to their barons. Thus three systems—mayor's courts, Puritan county courts, and feudal manorial courts—sat side by side in the colony of New York. On top of these dissimilar local courts, the Duke's Laws placed a general court of assize, meeting once each year and staffed by the governor, his council, and all the justices of the peace—the whole apparatus a compromise based on necessity and convenience.

The Duke's Laws did not end but rather began a period of rapid change in New York's legal structure. The colony's experience over the next three decades was a perfect example of the merger of public and private law. Every shift in English politics resulted in a shift in New York law. Partisan politics in the colony itself shaped and reshaped its laws. Successive governors, to fulfill their instructions and increase their authority, centralized, decentralized, and again centralized the legal system. At the end of the period, Jacob Leisler's rebellion totally destabilized New York politics and resulted in yet another recasting of the laws. When, in 1683, the English governors finally allowed an assembly to sit, the legislators not only considered questions of governance, but matters of private law as well.

After the period of rapid and confused experimentation between 1674 and 1691, the law and courts of the colony were partially Anglicized. A Supreme Court of Judicature brought with it a decisive turn toward adoption of the common law. True, the mayor's courts continued to function, particularly in New York City, and these courts were always more receptive to Roman law–based notions of commercial obligations. What is more, a "prerogative court," established in 1686 to hear disputes over wills, was unique in all the colonies. Nevertheless, after 1691, New York edged closer to the other colonies' structure of courts and law.

Pennsylvania law was a distinct variant of the colonial pattern from its inception because the first proprietor, William Penn, wanted his colony to be different. Penn owed this proprietary grant from the crown to his father's service as an admiral in the royal navy, the client-patron relationship behind most of the proprietary grants. The younger Penn had, unlike his father, converted to the Quaker faith, with its longing for inner spirituality and its rejection of war, pomp, the Mass, and the vestments of the established English church. Never a radical, Penn was soon a leading voice for moderation, order, and unity among the Quakers. When his grant was confirmed in 1681, Penn quickly moved to make his colony a haven for his co-religionists, including those Quakers long persecuted in Puritan New England and those already resident in the Quaker colonies of East and West Jersey. Among Quakers great and small in England and Wales, Penn quietly lobbied for support. He sold large tracts of land to the "first purchasers" but offered protection to the conscience and the rights of the least powerful would-be emigrant. His prospectus for the new colony became its Frame of Government, yet another example of the intimate tie between private and public law in the early colonies. In the Frame were elements of older grants but also a spark of Quaker egalitarianism that was unique.

The rights of inhabitants were fixed not by a vague injunction that the laws would be known and public, but by specific guarantees of rights that preceded and informed all exercise of government. Social misconduct, wantonness, and violence were punishable, but the penalties were far less severe than anywhere else in the king's domains. Most important, the political process was opened up to all Protestant religious persuasions, as was the right to worship in peace. The various frames of government, concessions, and grants of liberties that Penn issued during the 1680s, 1690s, and into the early eighteenth century contained what amounted to a bill of rights, including a guarantee of jury trial, counsel, and freedom from illegal search and seizure. The ill-usage of the Quakers in England by officers of the law bent on rooting out the sect influenced Penn's plan, as did a vision of a good society open to all peaceful emigrants.

The Quakers had always exhibited a love-hate relationship with the courts of law. Persecuted in English courts, Quakers fought back with lawsuits for assault, battery, and defamation against those who informed against them and those who broke into their meetinghouses. Quakers respected contracts and used trusts to protect their property against seizure by the crown. These were sophisticated legal artifices. Penn had no hesitation putting a judicial system into his first charter for the colony, but his courts and court procedure were less formal and criminal laws more forgiving than any in England or the colonies.

Pennsylvania had county courts of general jurisdiction, but for much of its existence it lacked a truly powerful central court structure. It gave to its justices of the peace the conventional range of regulatory and adjudicatory powers, its higher court judges heard appeals, and its assembly was a court of last resort (by petition), but the Quakers remembered the sting of persecution in the courts of England and were wary of giving too much power to their magistrates in the New World. Over time, the Quakers would lose control over the fate of Pennsylvania (Penn's son returned to the Church of England, and many non-Quakers migrated to the colony), and its laws would lose their distinctive moderate character.

Unlike the Puritans, the first Quaker arrivals did not have to deal with the warlike Mohawk of New York, the French-led Abenakis of Maine, or other aggressive tribes. Instead, the Quakers of Pennsylvania lived in peace and amity with the Lenape, or Delaware, Indians of the region. Penn's policy was legalistic in a wholly different way from that of the Puritans. Penn did not seek to use law to bilk or to rationalize injustice. Instead, his object was a good faith purchase of land from the heads of the tribe, followed by good faith dealings. Penn required "that all Differences between the Planters and the Natives shall also be ended by Twelve Men, that is by Six Planters and Six Natives, that so wee may Live friendly Together, and as much as in us Lyeth, Prevent all Occasions of Heart Burnings and Mischiefs."[4] This model of dispute resolution by arbitration was fair-minded, and long after Penn and the first settlers had died, many Indians so appreciated the Quaker policy that they went out of their way to protect the Quakers from the animosity of marauding war parties.

Like New York and Pennsylvania, the colonies of East Jersey and West Jersey were proprietary colonies. They began their legal existence as part of the land granted by Charles II to his brother James, the Duke of York, who passed them on to two friends, Lords Carteret and Berkeley. Berkeley, hard pressed for money to pay his debts, sold West Jersey to two Quakers. East Jersey remained a separate colony until its proprietor sold it to a consortium of Quakers. West Jersey, in reality the southern half of the present state of New Jersey, resembled Pennsylvania in its laws and courts. East Jersey, though Quakers had a controlling interest in land and government, was settled by a much more diverse and unruly population than West Jersey. There, Scots, Puritans, and Quakers did not get along, and the history of the colony was marked by civil strife. Its laws resembled those of Puritan New England. In 1702, the two Jerseys became a single royal colony, whose laws and courts thereafter became quite similar to those of New York.

When the middle colonies' courts diverged from patterns already established to the north and south, the former almost always had moved in the direction of even greater openness and receptivity to simple justice. By the early eighteenth century, the middle colonies had all but abandoned their experiment in legal innovation, but the marks of Quaker legal egalitarianism were still visible and still made a difference.

PROCEDURE

In the seventeenth century, an educated visitor in a colonial court might well hear many English legal "terms of art," but a plain style of pleading suits predominated. In Gloucester County, West Jersey, the proprietary courts of common pleas, sitting from 1686 through 1703, allowed parties to begin any actions with a writ of "case" and seek aid of the court through complaints and petitions framed in the plainest speech. In the records one occasionally finds a term of art, but often as not it is misused and almost always misspelled. Most often, litigants did not even bother to use the formulas of "writs." They simply went to the clerk of the court, paid for a summons that the sheriff delivered to the opposing party, came to court, and made a declaration of the facts. The only grounds for dismissing the suit was a substantial factual error in the plaintiff's pleading. If the plaintiff did not appear, the case was nonsuited. If the defendant failed to come, the plaintiff won by default. When both parties arrived for the sessions of the court, the case was then and there compromised, referred to arbitrators, or given to a jury. Until the middle 1690s, the vast majority of cases were handled in a single session of the court; thereafter most cases were continued for two sessions. The court gave relief in law and equity, making no distinction between those forms of redress.[5]

In the New York Supreme Court, arguably one of the most "English" courts in the colonies at the turn of the century, suits began and proceeded under the formalities of the English common law, but most of the cases were settled in one or two meetings of the court. There was little of the procedural maneuver that characterized sophisticated English civil pleading. Many of the same words of law that one found in formal pleading in the king's courts were intoned or written in the New York high court—Latin words and phrases conjoined in very old formulas—but the words were isolated markers of bits of legal learning, not evidence of the importation of an entire system of pleading.

Even these few terms of art were regarded with alarm by some colonial lawgivers. Thomas Lechford, an English legal scribe and solicitor who practiced law in Massachusetts from 1638 to 1641, found his niche writing very able technical pleas for submission to the Court of Assistants, but when he tried to impress his learning directly upon judges and juries, he was rebuffed and censured.[6] In 1705, Virginia planter and councillor (hence high-court judge) Robert Beverley defended the general jurisdiction and plain style of pleading in his colony's General Court against the criticism of newly arrived Governor Francis Nicholson. Nicholson, appalled by the loosely defined jurisdiction of his council, demanded the introduction of proper English legal etiquette. Beverley took the new governor's criticism personally and called Nicholson "a Man unacquainted with all Law, except that of Morocco, where he learnt the way of governing by force." Beverley thought Virginia's courts better off without English formalities: "They [parties and counsel in Virginia] used to come to the merits of the cause, as soon as they could without injustice, never admitted such impertinences of Form and Nicety, as were not absolutely necessary. . . . By this method, all fair Actions were prosecuted with little Attendance, all just Debts were recovered with the least expense of Money and Time; and all the Tricking and Foppery of the Law happily avoided."[7]

Expansive jurisdiction over subject matter and minimization of specialized and Latin pleading allowed local courts to resolve disputes without great expense in time or money and with a very few court officers. In the Springfield, Massachusetts, magistrates' court, William Pynchon could settle a defamation suit between John Woodcocke, Henry Gregory, and "Mr. Moxon" (the "Mr.," short for "Master," a mark of comparative status) by offering arbitration or jury trial and simultaneously threatening the parties with fines if they did not pay what they owed one another (the root cause of the slander). It did not matter to the parties or to Justice Pynchon that the case might have gone to the Assistants—they were in Boston, and the parties were in Springfield.[8]

The same informality and accessibility was the rule in southern courts in the seventeenth century. Late in the century, the Middlesex, Virginia, county court was held at Justice "Richard Robinson's mid-county house, just off the main road between its junction with the church path and the cutoff to the Piankatank ferry, [the county] paying Robinson twelve hundred pounds of tobacco yearly 'House Rent and Candle.'"[9] There was no courthouse, and men and women walked or rode the rutted, dusty path to Robinson's house to lay their claims before the justices. There might or might not be a lawyer present; ordinarily people spoke for themselves, though the paperwork had to be filed with the court clerk.

Procedure at the North Carolina Supreme Court in these years was not much different from a Virginia county court. "At a General Court Holden the 5th Day of October anno Domini 1697 at the house of Mr. Jonathan Godfrey" the deputy governor and the council of North Carolina approved the inventory of a deceased planter's estate, bound over Thomas Miller for contempt (he left the previous session of the court without permission), allowed Robert Munck 200 acres of land for bringing to the colony his wife and two servants (there were bounties of land to those who helped populate North Carolina), bound over Henry Palin for a "high misdemeanor" against the government (he criticized its conduct, and such criticism was a libel under English law), and then turned to civil suits. Richard Pope wanted his £24 (colony money, not sterling) from Richard Plater, but a jury impaneled on the spot found no merit in the suit. Pope was not done with Plater. The next day he brought suit against Plater for £38. 14s. 4d. on a "bill of exchange" (a precursor to the personal check), and this time the jury ordered Plater to pay 27 shillings, the outstanding debt. The court concluded its second day by listening to the Yawpin Indians complain against unscrupulous land speculators. The judges found merit in the Indians' claims and voided all grants of land within 3 miles of the Yawpin town.[10]

Although colonial lawmakers adopted in various ways the functions of the English courts of "equity," here, as in courts of law, procedure was simplified and relief made more accessible than in the English Court of Chancery. Equity, a parallel but distinct jurisprudential system to "law," was dispensed by chancellors who determined the facts in a suit through direct interrogation of parties and witnesses or written accounts (depositions) read into evidence in court. The chancellor could intervene in a lawsuit at any time in its process, enabling the parties to obtain relief not available at that time from courts of law. Parties could apply to the chancellor to compel their legal adversaries to produce documents, give testimony, and remain in the jurisdiction. Chancellors could enjoin or mandate that parties do or not do something—for example, not waste the assets of an estate until the legal issue of its ownership was settled or perform the terms of a contract. Parties to the suit disobeyed the chancellor at their peril. He had jurisdiction over their persons and could fine or imprison those who disobeyed his decrees. The chancellor of England was a learned judge, and process in his court was often long and costly as well as thoughtful and realistic.

In Maryland, New York, the Carolinas, Virginia, and New Jersey, the governor or the governor and his council were the chancellors. Their equity was swifter but less predictable than the work of the English chancellor. For a brief time, Pennsylvania experimented with a separate central court of equity. So did Rhode Island and New Hampshire, but these courts failed for political reasons. In Pennsylvania, Delaware, Massachusetts (until 1691), and Virginia, county justices performed the functions of chancellors. Local equity was plainly spoken, similar in outline to English equity but much less technical. The colonial assemblies of Massachusetts (until 1691), Connecticut, and Pennsylvania doubled as courts of equity, another example of the general jurisdiction common in American courts.

APPEALS

A corollary of the overlapping hierarchical structure, general jurisdiction, and of the relaxed rules of procedure in the first American courts was the right of appeal from a lower court to a higher one. In medieval English legal terminology, an "appeal" was a private individual's charge of felony against another private individual. Disputed civil cases could be carried back to the central courts when some point of law was unclear. There was no "right" to a civil appeal (the old writ of "right" was used to initiate an inquest into disputed land titles) in England in this period, though one could sue out a writ of error to bring a suit out of one court to another. The Court of King's Bench and Parliament regularly heard disputes on points of law initiated in other courts, but these were not appeals from the judgment of a lower court so much as suspension of deliberations in the lower court until it could be instructed in the law. One might appeal (that is, petition) for the chancellor to intervene, but this course of action took one out of the common-law courts.

Colonial supreme courts heard appeals of cases from the county courts on a regular basis. In most of the colonies, appeal entailed an entirely new trial of the facts, although the nominal basis for the appeal was ordinarily a disputed point of law. In this sense, colonial appeal was very different from the "appellate" jurisdiction of modern American courts. Today, appeal is based upon a claim that the lower court misstated the law. In the colonial courts, issues of law and fact were jumbled together, and appeal often turned on a new reading of factual submissions. For example, in 1671, William Mead and Ralph Ingram asked John Richards, a Boston lawyer, to bring suit against Ephraim Turner for £10 16s. sterling. Turner, a Boston merchant, ordered dry goods (linen and holland cloth) from Mead's and Ingram's shop in London, gave them a promissory note (in effect buying on credit with a fixed future date for repayment), and later refused to pay. Richards filed suit in the Suffolk county court but lost to the defense by Turner's brother, also a lawyer, that the note did not mention the person who might demand payment. Richards appealed to the Court of Assistants, whose judges instructed the jury differently about the law of merchants: the promissory note was negotiable; it was payable to the bearer upon demand. Turner then appealed to the next session of the Court of Assistants for a rehearing. He got it but did not prevail.[11]

A century later, local courts' findings were still subject to appeal to higher courts. In *Porter v. Steel* (1770–72), Asa Porter, a New Hampshire merchant, alleged that he had left with James Steel, a Massachusetts cooper with whom Porter had already done business, a sum to be paid to a third party, one Jacob Rowell. When Steel did not pay Rowell, Porter sued and won in county court on the argument that Steel had undertaken to do something and then did not do it. Steel appealed to the superior court when it came to Salem, in Essex County, insisting that Porter had not paid Steel anything to go to the trouble of giving the money to Rowell. He must also have convinced the jury at the superior court hearing that the receipt was for money that Porter previously owed Steel. Porter now sought and obtained a "writ of review" to return the suit to the supreme court, and in November 1772 the case was heard for the third time. A third jury reversed the verdict for Steel and ordered that he pay the sum back to Porter.[12] The right of appeal meant that the whole system of courts, with some limitations, was opened up to the lowliest suitor, though then as now burdens of expense and time prevented the poorest men and women from fully or frequently enjoying this right.

COURT OFFICIALS AND JUDGES

A third important distinction between colonial courts and English courts which promoted greater openness, lay in the training of personnel. True, the workhorse of the system, the English justice of the peace, was not very different in status, recruitment, and outlook from the colonial local magistrate. In Massachusetts, for example, lay justices of the peace like John Clark of Suffolk County were able men, respected in their communities, who tempered the rigor of the law with concern for the individual situation of the accused, just as justices of the peace in Suffolk County, England, did. Clark handled both civil and minor criminal matters with dispatch, relying on the "watch and warn" system of recognizance that marked English and New England local justice. Clark and the other justices (some eighteen for the county) were also the first line of enforcement of the regulatory statutes, fining violators, warning out potential paupers, and keeping the peace. Not so respected or effective were the lay local justices of North Carolina, where one-tenth of the county bench were at one time or another called to account for misconduct. Neither were justices of the colony's superior court always treated with respect by their neighbors: in October 1771, rioters disrupted a superior court session and covered the judge's chair with manure.[13]

Unlike the justices of the peace, the officials of the courts in England and the judges of the king's high courts were very different from the colonial court clerks and supreme court judges. The clerks of the English courts of King's Bench, Common Pleas, Exchequer, and Chancery were well trained in the law. Many had practiced law themselves and sought appointment as "prothonotaries" (chief clerks) or underclerks in the central courts because the fees due them in these positions could be quite substantial. English court clerks oversaw the issuing and recording of official documents and supervised the flow of litigation. They were much respected and vital cogs in the machinery of the legal system.

Colonial governors made brave statutory attempts to transplant the English court clerk to the colonies, but in the main this vital infrastructure of English court practice did not reappear in the colonies. In 1707, Lieutenant Governor John Evans of Pennsylvania and his adviser Robert Assheton drafted a statute calling for "the office of the clerk or prothonotary of the supream court . . . [to issue legal documents] as fully and amply to all intents and purposes as . . . the Court of Queens Bench, Comon Pleas, and Exchequer, at Westminster."[14] Prothonotaries were to sit at the county courts as well. Despite a generous fee schedule (which the assembly almost immediately reduced) and the prospect of immense discretion in managing the local courts' day to day affairs, most prothonotaries subsequently appointed were not men of legal learning. Instead, the office became a patronage plum for cronies of the governor, in effect his loyal eyes and ears in the counties. Throughout the first colonies, clerkships of court ordinarily went not to a professionally trained administrative cadre, but to relatives, supporters, and friends of powerful judges and governors.

Like the prothonotaries who served them, English judges were full-time professional jurists, and though almost invariably advanced in their careers because of their political allegiances, they were almost always well trained and much experienced in the law. Colonial high-court judges were laymen of affairs and authority in their communities who were acquainted with law but rarely trained in it. Moreover, they were never full-time jurists. After three-quarters of a century of operation, the highest courts of Massachusetts and Virginia rarely included more than one well-educated lawyer. The legal skills of the judges in Pennsylvania were no higher. Only the Duke of York's province could boast a legally literate bench. This pattern continued well into the eighteenth century in most of the colonies.

The result of laymen on the high-court benches might be, as Robert Beverley believed, swift and sensible justice. Massachusetts superior court justices like Samuel Sewall were deeply moral men, concerned about the quality of their performance. Sewall was typical of the best lay judges—well traveled, well schooled, much respected, and experienced in colonial government and in hearing and deciding lawsuits, if not learned in the law. His diary and the records of the Superior Court of Judicature while he sat on its bench from 1692 to 1728 show an able and sensible magistrate—with one terrifying exception. That exception demonstrated the danger posed by lay judges. In the Salem witchcraft trials of 1692 the judges, including Sewall, unsure of their discretion to depart from English practice, did so with tragic consequences.

Against the advice of almost all the Puritan ministers of the colony, the judges decided to admit into testimony spectral evidence, the uncorroborated testimony of adolescent girls that they had been visited and tormented by otherwise invisible wraiths. In fact, the quarrel that led to their "possession" by witches was mundane, a tangled web of mistrust and animosity between agricultural Salem Village and more prosperous, commercial Salem Town. The inhabitants of Salem Village wanted to retain the services of Minister Samuel Parris. The ratepayers of Salem Town had not wanted the village to have its own church in the first place and by 1691 were opposed to Parris's retention. Quarrels over the retention of ministers were common in New England towns, but this one was carried on with great venom because it overlay a struggle between the two most powerful families in Salem, the Putnams of the village and the Porters of the village and town. To their quarrel in 1691 was added the sudden hysteria of a handful of adolescent girls, excited by the tales of witchcraft spun by Parris's West Indian servant, Tituba. The girls were all associated with the Parris-Putnam faction (one of the girls was Parris's daughter). Carol Karlsen has taken a second look at these "possessed" young women and found that many of them had lost one or both of their parents and had little prospect of making good marriages or inheriting property from their families. The young women, facing the traumas of sexual identification in a society whose male authorities limited what women could do and be, may well have experienced a collective "profound conflict."[15] Local factionalism focused their accusations on the Porters and their friends, the persecutors of Samuel Parris. When well-meaning Puritan ministers tried to help the girls, the ministers inadvertently manufactured the witchcraft crisis. Frightened by the hideous shapes of their own imaginings, the preachers turned to the lay judges to scourge the witches.

For the authorities, Salem's troubles became a microcosm of the ills of the colony, for the colony itself seemed under a malign spell. For rising up against royal Governor Edmund Andros in 1689, Massachusetts had lost its old charter of government and feared for its continued existence. To many devout Puritans, it seemed that the Devil was abroad and doing mischief.

In the late spring of 1692, Governor William Phips returned from England, where he had tried unsuccessfully to regain the old system of government for his colony, to find the jails of Essex County filled with suspected witches. Temporarily without a charter, he had no power to convene a court to hear the charges. Indeed, even under the proposed new charter, courts had to be created by the legislature of the colony, and the legislature would not meet until the end of the year. Faced with the crisis, he used his discretion to fashion a special court. To its bench were named laymen like Sewall, former Assistants like Nathaniel Saltonstall, ambitious politicians like William Stoughton, the lieutenant governor, and local justices like John Hathorne (whose descendant Nathaniel Hawthorne would movingly re-create the terror of the trial) and Jonathan Corwin. There were no trained lawyers on the bench. Wary that their proceedings would be criticized, the judges tried to follow the letter of English criminal procedure. At the same time, they were the conscious representatives of a Puritan way of life that was under fire. The result was that they allowed every woman who confessed to witchcraft to escape punishment in order to demonstrate that a contrite heart was essential to Puritan justice, and they sentenced to death women who were undoubtedly innocent of anything except the enmity of a handful of adolescent girls.

Saltonstall was so appalled at the work of the court that he quietly resigned from the bench before any of the women were executed. By the end of the proceedings, nineteen women were hanged for witchcraft and one old man crushed to death under stones for refusing to plead to a charge, all upon evidence the court could neither see nor test but accepted. Over a hundred more awaited trial or execution of sentence when Governor Phips abruptly canceled the court's special commission.

Five years after the trials, one week after burying his own young sons, Sewall asked forgiveness of God and man for the tragedy of the Salem trials: "Samuel Sewall, sensible of the reiterated stroke of God upon himself and family; and being sensible, that as to the Guilt contracted, upon the opening of the late Commission of Oyer and Terminer at Salem [the special court that tried and condemned the suspects] he is, upon many accounts, more concerned than any that he knows of, Desires to take the Blame and Shame of it, Asking Pardon of men."[16] Sewall would later inveigh against slavery and call for fair treatment of Indians. For his part, Stoughton never looked back.

LAWYERS

A modern reader of the Salem witchcraft trial records would surely ask why the defendants' lawyers did not object to the judges' hectoring of witnesses and admission of spectral evidence. The answer is that no one trained in law "represented" the accused. There were lawyers in Massachusetts, but the establishment and operation of legal systems in the seventeenth-century colonies was accomplished with only sporadic intervention by professional lawyers. True, the crown's legal advisers drafted the charters of the companies and the proprietaries, and the king's attorney general and solicitor general sat in the Privy Council and reviewed colonial laws. A few lawyers even came to the new colonies, but they did not play a major role in lawmaking or law enforcement. Recent scholarship has found more and more lawyers, lawyer-gentlemen, particularly in the southern colonies, and lawyer-merchants in the North, but the profession of law did not assert itself in the colonies until the eighteenth century.

The paucity of lawyers in the seventeenth-century colonies is all the more striking because of the increasing eminence and influence of lawyers in England. The rise of the bar in the fifteenth century was coincidental with a rising passion for litigation. As E. W. Ives observed, "English society was intensely 'law-minded,' obsessed with legal considerations, legal rights and legal remedies. . . . English men—and women—went to law with alacrity."[17] Some might disparage local attorneys as the "vipers" and "pettifoggers" of the land, but the demand for legal services made lawyering profitable. Attorneys managed estates, wrote wills, and advised clients on all manner of business.

At the top of the profession of law, very able lawyers gravitated to the central courts in Westminster. There, potent common-law practitioners had been the "serjeants" at law, chosen by the crown, educated at the Inns of Court, and tabbed for high-court judgeships. In the seventeenth century these men gave pride of place to the newly created "king's counsel." In the courts of equity, solicitors and barristers both plied their trade, and in the ecclesiastical and admiralty courts labored the "civilians," so called because the source of church and admiralty law was the civil law of Rome. A guild of "scriveners" prepared legal documents and bitterly fought off attempts to dismantle their near monopoly. Although the distinction was not locked in place until the next century, "barristers," former students of the Inns of Court called to the "bar," pleaded in the common-law courts, but they could not solicit legal business or exact fees. Barristers worked on cases supplied by "solicitors."

Despite the flowering of the legal profession in England, the seventeenth-century colonists were wary of lawyers, and few came to the early colonies. A full three decades after the founding of the Maryland colony, George Alsop quipped: "Here if the lawyer had nothing else to maintain him but his bawling, he might button up his Chops, and burn his Buckrom Bag . . . then with a Spade, like his Grandsire Adam, turn up the face of Creation, purchasing his bread by the sweat of his brows."[18] Lawyers were no more welcome in Penn's colony. As Gabriel Thomas wrote in 1698: "Of lawyers . . . I shall say nothing, because this country is very peaceable . . . long may it so continue and never have occasion for the tongue of the [lawyer] . . . destructive of mens estates and lives."[19]

In Massachusetts, Thomas Lechford complained that no attention was paid to the niceties of law. He meant that a lawyer could not make a living pleading in court. The Massachusetts General Court, at first, did not even permit a lawyer to earn a fee for advocacy. The Puritans were much attracted to law but had no liking for lawyers. As the number of attorneys—men representing others in court—increased slowly but steadily, the General Court finally recognized the inevitable by allowing lawyers to sue "in any of our courts." In 1702, the General Court further conceded that counsel could exact 12 shillings per suit, "and no more."[20] In Virginia, a 1643 statute limited fees for representing a client to 20 pounds of tobacco and required that the lawyers be licensed and sworn. The penalty for overcharging a client was 500 pounds of tobacco.[21]

Georgia, the youngest of the colonies, resisted the advances of the lawyers. In December 1733, Governor James Oglethorpe reported to the trustees of the colony that "every man pleads his own cause." The next year, Samuel Eveleigh reported from the colony that "Causes were try'd (and in my Judgement) very impartially, without the Jargon or the confused Quirks of the Lawyer's and without any Cost or Charges, and Yet (in my Opinion) consonant to reason and Equity, which I take to be the foundation of all laws." Alas for this Edenic idyll, the lawyers found their way to Georgia as soon as the charitable trusteeship gave way to a royal colony.[22]

Even where legislatures allowed lawyers to practice, they limited what lawyers could earn from a case. Soon after they got the right to charge for their pleading in court, lawyers lost the right to bargain with their clients for payment—a right they did not regain until the middle of the nineteenth century. Instead, assemblies promulgated fee schedules. In some colonies lawyers (as well as judges, court clerks, and other officers of the court) were paid by the plea, literally by the pieces of paper filed with the courts. In New Jersey, the fee for a summons was 6 pence and the fee for all actions tried "to the bench" was 3 shillings. The attorney general of the colony got 15 shillings for prosecuting a criminal case, twice that amount if the offense was capital. In Maryland the fees were set by law and paid in hogsheads of tobacco until a 1733 statute provided for payment in money.

THE REGULATORY ACTS

A final piece of English law washed up on the American shore and was transformed here by social necessities. Elizabethan and early Stuart Parliaments engaged in a veritable frenzy of regulatory lawmaking. Nearly every session of Parliament enacted new statutes to control domestic conduct and economic activity. Prices were regulated, as was the gold thread in one's clothing, the language of one's prayers, the occupation one could follow, and the profits one could make. Statutes of Artificers fixed wages, and Poor Laws set up workhouses for the indigent. The relations between master and apprentice, servant and employer, and husband and wife were regulated as well. At the heart of the entire program was a moral agenda: social conformity, religious obedience, and hard work—in part the reflection of the Protestant vision of a nation of busy bees, in part a reaction to the increasing numbers of poor people on the roads looking for work. Our modern regulatory state may have grown out of the New Deal in the 1930s, but the Elizabethan state, the Tudor monarchy in England, was far more regulatory than the modern state.

The same statutory language, read in different physical surroundings in the New World, resulted in unexpected consequences. American authorities tried to replicate English regulatory laws and ended up with a system far closer to William Penn's than James I's. As Richard B. Morris demonstrated in *Government and Labor in Early America* (1946), much of the statute law of regulation came in one form or another to the colonies impelled by the same social impulse—the desire of an elite to control the supposedly wayward behavior of the laboring classes (though the acts did not use the language of "class" at all). Economic and geographic conditions in the colonies undermined the intentions of the early colonial lawmakers. It was impossible for guilds to emerge, much less gain a monopoly over trades, for masters to hold on to apprentices, and for wage and price controls to work when there was so much economic and geographic mobility in the colonies. Scarcity of labor—hence the relatively powerful bargaining position of free labor in the colonies—hamstrung social and economic controls.

To be sure, there were exceptions. When local magnates could import labor from England, as the Pynchons did in Springfield, Massachusetts, in the first fifty years of the colony, bound laborers were worse off here than in their countries of origin. West African men and women were surely freer before Arab slavers brought them to the coast and sold them into bondage in America. Nevertheless, for many ordinary Americans, high wages and occupational opportunity created a very fluid social and economic structure.

When regulation in the colonies was effective, it was not because of the fiat of central authorities but because local authorities determined to enforce the regulations. In Massachusetts, whose regulations were the most precise and the most voluminous in the colonies, the towns regulated the admission of newcomers, the division of land, and entry to occupations very effectively until the end of the seventeenth century. Wages were higher in Massachusetts than in England and the treatment of servants much improved, but attempts to limit profits were not successful. In the middle colonies, initial attempts to regulate the economy and social status failed when local authorities could not enforce the rules, but they succeeded when the populace benefited from the regulations. For example, soon after 1700, "Philadelphia and New York operated carefully regulated public markets where foodstuffs and many nonperishable items were sold by schedule several times a week."[23]

Regulatory legislation worked well in the southern colonies—for example, regulation of the tobacco industry was rigorously enforced. At weighing stations, inspectors graded and weighed hogsheads of tobacco and stamped its value on receipts. So important were these tobacco receipts to the economy of the colony that they circulated as a paper currency. Forgery of tobacco certificates was made a felony, though it went on with great frequency. The treatment and duties of servants and slaves were also minutely prescribed, though the latter had little precedent in English statutes.

The End of Isolation

The elaboration of the "American difference" in the seventeenth century was possible only because England's rulers had their hands full with noble plotters, sectarian rebels, and all manner of foreign enemies. Fitfully, the Stuarts had tried to reassert their control over their colonial domains, but their efforts did not strike home until James II demolished the New England charter colonies of Massachusetts, Rhode Island, and Connecticut and pressed the pieces together into the ill-conceived and short-lived "Dominion of New England." When James was driven from his throne in the "Glorious Revolution," his schemes for colonial governance were violently rejected in the colonies themselves. The ironic result was closer scrutiny of colonial laws. David Lovejoy has pointed out that "in several ways the abrupt changes cleared the air; they forced [colonial] leaders and followers to do some thinking about bases upon which they could build interim—maybe permanent—governments. . . . there was a good deal of talk and speculation about equitable foundations and workable guarantees for protecting rights and liberties, civil and religious, which they had rebelled to recover, or in some instances, discover."[24] Brief uprisings in North America led to heightened scrutiny of the imperial system by James II's successors in Westminster. In fits and starts, the law in the colonies was more carefully sifted by lawyers for the home government and made more consonant with English law.

To be sure, this project had precedent. Crown lawyers had stood at the elbow of the first proprietors as the charters and grants for the very first settlements passed through the royal "seals." Later, lawyers for the Lord Protector, Oliver Cromwell, fleshed out the first statutes regulating colonial trade, the beginning of the myriad of "Navigation Acts" defining the economics of empire. Lawyers for Charles II, when he was restored to his throne in 1660, assisted Parliament in extending the Navigation Acts to all manner of subjects, preventing the colonists from competing with English manufacturers as well as requiring the colonists to send their staple crops to England. Lawyers for King William and Queen Mary after 1689 took a system that had worked by fits and starts and gave it bureaucratic structure, continuity, and order. In this newly rationalized administrative context, legal formalities would become far more important than they had been.

Flushed with their part in the toppling of obnoxious King James II, colonial assemblymen thought themselves capable of creating courts and defining their jurisdiction without help from the crown. The result, as in Virginia, was confusion. One critic, possibly Robert Beverley of Virginia, anonymously complained in an English pamphlet:

> It is a great Unhappiness, that no one can tell what is Law, and what is not, in the Plantations; some hold that the Law of *England* is chiefly to be respected, and where that is deficient, the Laws of the several colonies are to take place; others are of Opinion, that the Laws of the Colonies are to take first place, and that the law of *England* is of force only where they [colonial law] are silent . . . . Thus we are left in the dark, in one of the most considerable Points of our Rights.[25]

The king's Privy Council, advised by the king's attorney general and solicitor general, looked askance at any exercise of American independent-mindedness. Colonial acts creating courts were meticulously scrutinized in England and nullified when the colonists tried to diverge from English practice. For example, soon after William and Mary ascended to the throne, Massachusetts' attempts to create courts that were independent of royal favor were twice struck down, along with provisions for counsel in criminal trials. In later years, the Privy Council regularly acted as a court of last resort in colonial lawsuits. The legal isolation of the American colonies was over.

When relatively isolated from the mother country, the colonists developed legal systems that suited their needs and dispensed with English formalities. Some American reforms took root; others failed to survive.

Public and private law remained closely intertwined. The seventeenth century was hardly a golden age of American law, as the Salem witch-craft trials amply demonstrated, but it was an era in which American law was more independent of English law than it would be for nearly another century.

CHAPTER THREE

"These Dirty and Ridiculous Litigations

Have Been Multiplied in this Town,

Till the Very Earth Groans and

the Stones Cry Out"

L aw, Judge Richard Posner has written, serves three functions. It defines the power of government and the rights of citizens; it keeps order; and it provides the framework for the resolution of disputes.[1] In Chapter Two, we considered colonial law "from above"—as the structure of governance of new communities in a New World. For the colonist, such public lawmaking was part and parcel of everyday life, for the colonists created their governments at the same time as they plowed their fields, reared their children, and sought salvation in their churches. They did not, however, rush to court at every opportunity to use the organs of public authority to resolve private disputes—not, at least, at first.

Informal Dispute Resolution

In the first colonial settlements, the formal lawsuit was more often than not a last resort. Colonists did not shun their courts, but alternatives to courts of common law and criminal justice mediated between the community and the individual. Order keeping and dispute resolution were social activities. For example, members of early New England churches would subject themselves and their quarrels to the arbitration of the elders of the church. In 1640, Richard Wayte, a Boston tailor accused of stealing "buckskin lether," protested his innocence before civil courts but confessed his sins and professed his contrition when the First Church of Boston threatened to excommunicate him. The Quakers of Pennsylvania and New Jersey brought all manner of quarrels and accusations to their church courts. Mere physical or hearsay evidence was not allowed to stand without confirmation from witnesses. Over time, formalities borrowed from the courts of law began to creep into Quaker proceedings, giving them a legalistic cast. Well into the eighteenth century, however, Quaker church courts heard cases that would today be classified as civil wrongs (torts), violations of regulatory statutes, breaches of contract, and charges of immorality. Often the church court would arrange mediation, which the parties voluntarily accepted. Until the end of the seventeenth century, the vestries of Anglican parishes in the southern colonies doubled as courts to settle allegations of immorality and personal vituperation. The vestry, like the New England town, also arranged for the hiring, salary, and dismissal of ministers, a task that involved much negotiation and compromise but sometimes led to court action of a more formal sort.

Even when a dispute led to the steps of the courthouse, alternatives to trial were available. All parties willing, the case might be "referred" to arbitrators, knowledgeable and respected neighbors who would bring their decision back to the court. This was common among merchants in New Amsterdam under the Dutch and later New York City under the English, the Puritans of New England, the planters of the Tidewater, and the Quakers who settled Pennsylvania and New Jersey. Referral of cases to arbitrators, sometimes lawyers but more often men of status in the neighborhood, regularly occurred in all the colonies. Such arbitration was not final, but a way to avert a lawsuit. David Konig has offered evidence that this system was beginning to buckle in the last decades of the seventeenth century. In Essex County, Massachusetts, "one of the most important and frequently used methods of conflict resolution . . . had been local arbitration." Between 1672 and 1692 the county court heard and determined forty-five suits that arbitrators had failed to resolve.[2]

The failure of arbitration in any particular case did not mean that arbitration disappeared. Referral to arbitrators was often joined to trial by jury. When New Jersey Quakers Edward Eglington and his wife, Sarah, brought a slander suit against Samuel Harrison and his wife, another Quaker family, a jury in Gloucester County found the Harrisons guilty and awarded the Eglingtons 5 pence damages. The same jury heard the Harrisons' suit for slander (the words do not bear repetition in print, though it is remarkable how much more graphic seventeenth-century cursing is than modern vituperation) against the

Eglingtons and found for the Harrisons. Instead of executing judgment according to the verdicts upon the two couples, the justices bound them to the peace and ordered them to return to the next session of court. Meanwhile the justices put pressure on both families to end their caterwauling. It was unseemly and untoward for Quakers to carry on spiteful quarrels in public. The justices' methods worked: after six months the Eglingtons and the Harrisons agreed "to submitt themselves and agree to leave ye determination of all controversies and differences whatsoever between ye parties" to the "decision and determination of Thomas Thackera, Samuel Spicer, John Wood, and James Atkinson." Spicer was a judge on the very court that heard both suits; Wood was the county coroner; Thackera was a member of the grand jury. The entire system—magistrates, juries, arbitrators—came into play to prevent a neighborly spat from becoming something more ominous.[3]

In predominantly local economies, worlds of barter of goods and services, neighbors dealt with neighbors. When neighbors called one another cheats, threw one another's wigs into tavern fireplaces, and tore down one another's fences, seventeenth-century courts arranged for settlements within the intimacy of communal understandings. Most cases were heard and disposed of in a single sitting of the court, sometimes through the intervention of arbitrators. Everyone knew everyone else. Juries of neighbors, often leading men in the community who dealt with the parties on a regular basis outside of court and knew a good deal about their quarrel, gave community sanction to verdicts for one side or the other. Civil litigation in this context was a final chapter of a story that wove its way through months and years of shifting personal contacts. Courts reinforced the ties of family, work, and status which already existed in a community.

Predictably, the status and reputation of the parties mattered in court. As William Offutt, Jr., proves in his splendid study of the Quaker communities on both sides of the Delaware River, "though access to a court was theoretically equal to all, in practice those with power in this legal system," the magistrates themselves or their kin, "used the courts disproportionately often to solve their problems." Indeed, "the relationship between land, office, and wealth, on the one hand, and litigants on the other can be expressed in a few straightforward sentences. If you sued, you were on average better off [in socioeconomic status] than those who did not sue. If you sued a lot, you were better off still." The better off a party was, the more likely he was to participate in all the activities of the legal system. Finally, those who were best off were usually able to persuade lower status parties to settle out of court.[4]

Later in the century, the powerful continued to dominate in the Jersey courts. Poorer landowners had great difficulty resisting the land hunger of greedy speculators because of the "staggering cost of battling [wealthy] proprietary lawsuits."[5] Only by combining their resources could farmers keep speculators at bay, but what would happen in this system if many outsiders—merchants from across the ocean, for example—brought suit or more quarrels focused on forms of property and types of transactions whose value derived not from common, local understandings but from abstract legal relationships?

The First Litigation Explosion

In the eighteenth century the number of lawsuits in colonial courts began to increase much more rapidly than the increase in population (itself growing markedly), with the result that the "rate" of litigation spiraled upward—a veritable explosion of litigation. Rates leveled off for a time, but the litigiousness of ordinary colonists had become a fixture of colonial legal landscape. As John Adams said of his own Braintree, "these dirty and ridiculous Litigations have been multiplied in this Town, till the very Earth groans and the stones cry out."[6]

Behind the surge was a deeper change in society—a "sea change" in the way some colonists did business with one another. Over the course of the eighteenth century, the opening of internal markets and the spread of a money economy affected individual thinking about disputes and ended in civil litigiousness. In this surge of civil suits, the line between private actions and public causes remained indistinct, in part because some of the most litigious members of these communities were politicians and some of the most important suits involved government action.

The New England courts were the first to feel the impact of the sea change in litigation rates. Rates of litigation in colonial courts can only be regarded as approximations, but evidence from New England records reveals an explosion of litigiousness in the early eighteenth century. Peter Russell documented the surge of litigiousness in the Massachusetts Superior Court of Judicature between 1710 and 1730: there was a 226.8 percent increase in the number of suits filed. By 1730, the rate of lawsuits per thousand people had leapt to three times the level of 1700. Thereafter, the litigation rate remained stable. In four sessions of the Plymouth County, Massachusetts, court of common pleas held in 1703, there were 16 cases on the docket. By 1717, there were 97. In 1727 this had increased to 140. In 1730, the number stood at 385. In 1733, the caseload had declined to 245. It continued to decline through the middle of the century; by 1762, it stood at 215, a figure close to that for the rest of the colonial period. Throughout the century, the Plymouth population rose, but the litigiousness in the 1720s and early 1730s outran population. In 1730, there were filed 8 suits for every 100 adults in the county.

Fairly steep rises in litigation rates over fairly short periods of time were too common in the first half of the 1700s to be accidental or co-incidental. The towns of Gloucester and Marblehead, Massachusetts, experienced an upsurge of litigation between 1710 and the middle 1730s, as did Hartford County, Connecticut. In 1740, the Hartford County, Connecticut, courts were inundated with 1,632 suits, of which 1,520 involved debts of some kind. Hartford County contained no more than 15,000 or so adults, giving a litigation rate for debt alone of 10 for every 100 adults.

New England was not alone in experiencing this rage for litigation. Caseloads in Richmond County, Virginia, grew ahead of population in the early eighteenth century, and docket entries for courts in Glouces-ter County, New Jersey, rose steeply between 1715 and 1730—far out of proportion to the increase in population. The New York Supreme Court heard twelve times as many cases in the middle 1750s as it did in the 1690s, while population only increased sixfold. There is no evidence that a decline in the caseloads of other courts in the colony led to the increase in the high court's caseload, but scholars have not yet deter-mined whether the number of cases in the 1750s was a high point in a steady growth of litigation.

The vast majority of all these lawsuits claimed that the defendant had failed to pay a debt or honor a contractual obligation. The colonial economic system ran on credit—credit extended from British mer-chants to American merchants, credit extended from British commodi-ties importers to American wheat farmers and rice and tobacco plan-ters, credit the local shopkeeper extended to his or her neighbors. After the European wars of the "Spanish Succession," ending in 1713, Euro-pean demand for important colonial staples such as wheat, tobacco, and sugar slid into a temporary decline. Prices tumbled. The shock waves of economic recession passed through England to the colonies, but debt itself was nothing new to the colonists. There had been sharp contractions of the economy after every colonial war, and every con-traction set in motion the same pattern of bankruptcy and debt. None before had led to such a persistent and deeply rooted march to the courthouse steps, however. The question thus remains, Why did more colonists than ever before take their quarrels over indebtedness to the courts?

Some scholars suspect that this surge of litigation can be attributed to the rise of a cadre of lawyers who instigated suits for their own financial gain. In this, the scholars track the anti-lawyer sentiments often expressed by colonists. In fact, most colonies had statutes barring lawyers from instigating suits. Lawyers undoubtedly stirred up some business on their own, but the arrival of the lawyers did not bring a marked increase in litigiousness. In Gloucester City, New Jersey, for example, and in Richmond County, Virginia, lawyers were appearing for clients for decades before the litigation rates skyrocketed. Lawyers did not create the litigation explosion; the reverse is true. The growth of litigation began in the 1710s and 1720s and drew men into the profession. The litigators followed the litigants into court. The emergence of law as a profitable profession resulted from changing expectations of litigants, though by no means did every plaintiff and every defendant in a lawsuit seek the aid of professional counsel. In 1760, the ratio of lawsuits filed by lawyers to suits filed by the parties themselves in Massachusetts counties such as Worcester and Hampshire was about one to ten and one to nine, respectively. There is a far more nuanced and complex explanation for the surge in litigation at the beginning of the eighteenth century.

COMMERCE AND LITIGATION

The explanation begins with large-scale events, great and deep changes in the structures of colonial economic life, but does not stop with such generalizations. To be convincing, any explanation of the increasing popularity of going to law must reach down to the individual potential plaintiff and potential defendant.

As more and more of the American towns and parishes became enmeshed in the interpersonal dynamics of world trade, a larger and larger number of disputes over commerce turned into formal lawsuits. When residents of different towns, counties, parishes, or colonies began to contest one another's claims, and their quarrels more and more often concerned impersonal instruments of commercial dealing such as bills of exchange and promissory notes, litigation ceased to be the last chapter in a communal story and became the introduction to a detached, abstract legal episode.

The New England experience is instructive and worth a second, harder look. The broader context of change in this bygone world— shifts in the legal culture and its values, ways of doing business and dealing with neighbors—is clear. Bit by bit, the isolation of New England towns and the discipline of church and town meetings broke down, and New Englanders turned to the courts to resolve differences among themselves. The gradual intrusion of a money economy, of trade with strangers "at arm's length," undercut alternatives to litigation in the courts. The rise of busy and relatively impersonal commercial centers increased the number and complexity of transactions among strangers. Subsistence-farming villages were drawn into a network of commercial farms clustered around growing towns. The legal system responded to the expansion of commerce. "Debt litigation became formalistic and unforgiving, pleading grew more technical and less expressive of the facts of individual disputes, and the civil jury faded from predominance to comparative insignificance. . . . the changes marked a transformation from a legal system that allowed litigants to address their grievances in ways that were essentially communal to one that elevated predictability and uniformity of legal relations over responsiveness to individual communities. . . . Notes and bonds gave credit transactions an intrinsic predictability that rested on legal form rather than on trust." Even arbitration became a legally enforceable remedy.[7]

The growing importance of commercial paper—promissory notes, bonds, and bills of exchange—in the web of credit which stretched across the face of New England commerce subtly but critically altered the place of women in the courts. In the less formal atmosphere of seventeenth-century indebtedness, women were fully if not equally engaged in keeping the accounts books for the family farm or business. They initiated and testified regularly in "book debt" cases. Indeed, in New Haven County, Connecticut, from 1666 to 1720, women were the plaintiffs in 15 percent of the debt suits brought to the county court. After 1720, women's participation in such litigation declined steeply; over the course of the next two decades, women only brought ninety-five debt actions. Cornelia Dayton has examined these cases in detail and concluded that women were simply not as involved in the making or contesting of negotiable instruments as they were in book debt actions. "The commercializing trends that made New Haven a bustling, prosperous port by 1760 did not signal a drastic curtailment in the daily, face-to-face trading activities in which New England women had always engaged. . . . But by the 1770s the dominant economy had broken out of local bounds. Credit relations became cash-infused, impersonal, and dependent on written instruments. Although New England women continued to play a crucial role in household management, the worlds of commerce and credit in which their menfolk partook were increasingly unknown and alien to them."[8] The decline of women coming to court to pursue their debtors mirrored the declining importance of the household economy in the wider world of business.

DIGNITY AND LITIGIOUSNESS

One certainly can explain increasing rates of litigation in terms of changing social and economic forces—large-scale events involving many people. In most of the cases, an economic transaction had gone wrong. When many colonists found themselves enmeshed in disputes over new forms of property and unfamiliar types of transactions, often involving strangers, the courts of law were the only place where the parties' rights and duties could be determined.

The grand changes in the way the colonists did business, and with whom, framed the outer contours of the litigation explosion, but they do not explain why individuals decided that no recourse was open to them in a dispute but a lawsuit. The surge in litigation can be seen as a shifting of the border between such disputes and actual lawsuits. Why did proportionately more people insist that disputes be taken to court in the 1720s and 1730s than in the 1700s? Why did they press their claims (as a plaintiff) or resist the claims of another person (as a defendant) in larger numbers in the 1720s and 1730s than they had in prior decades?

At the heart of a lawsuit is a sense of wronged dignity, of damaged personal self-worth. One stops disputing and starts suing when one believes that one's opponent denigrates one's credibility and diminishes one's status in the community. Dignity is social: the mirror the community holds up to men and women, in which they see their personal value. For plaintiffs and defendants in court, personal dignity became social consciousness; their opponents had broken the rules that held the community together and must be chastised publically. The lawsuit is thus an exchange of visible signs—words, gestures, pieces of paper—a public conversation among the parties carried out in front of the community. Such events are dramatic dialogues, in which the parties are principals and the neighbors act as chorus and audience.

Litigation expresses a plaintiff's sense that the community itself is imperiled by the defendant's conduct. The plaintiff comes to believe that he or she speaks for the community when he or she brings suit in its courts. For their part, defendants force the issue because they believe that their rights are the rights of everyone around them; they hold fast for the sake of the community as well as for their own. Individualized in this way, rises in litigation rates not only reflect societal influences upon groups of potential litigants but also express individual litigants' attempts to restate and reinforce the social values of their society. Civil litigation enables an entire community to explore and test the boundaries of personal conduct. When the boundaries become indistinct or too many people seem to be crossing the boundaries, litigation will increase. When the values of a community are under attack or are changing too rapidly for potential litigants—plaintiffs or defendants—to control, men and women will troop to the courts to reassert traditional, unwritten rules.

In the light of these suggestions about personal dignity, social values, and civil litigation, one can see more deeply into the causes of the litigation explosion of the early eighteenth century. Lawsuits multiplied when more potential plaintiffs sensed that they had not only been wronged, but that their community needed them to bring that wrong to court. When a changing economy threatened communal values, potential plaintiffs grew anxious that potential defendants were trying to get away with something. Potential defendants themselves, bewildered by the speed and scope of economic and social changes, resisted confession of their supposed delicts and debts or referral of the disputes to arbitration. They resented what seemed to them to be plaintiffs' suddenly unreasonable demands. The defendants forced a day in court to prevent the plaintiff from breaking the old rules.

In the period from 1710 to 1730 when litigation rates first surged, the long-term expansion of commerce and its instrumentalities—combined with the growing breakdown of traditional institutions of social control—created a crisis of social values. In the two decades when new ways of doing business first gained the approval of the courts, but neighbors still believed that strangers were using law to violate older norms of conduct, the courts' dockets began to grow full. Litigiousness swelled during this phase change, a temporary disparity between new and old social norms. For example, New York's overcrowded supreme court dockets in this period mirrored the struggle between a new commercial elite, tied to the crown, and a corps of artisans and small landholders. The courts became one battleground for these forces as artisan and yeoman debtors struck back at wealthy merchants and landlords. When a new alliance of artisans, yeomen, and anticrown elite families, principally the Livingstons, formed in the 1760s, the litigation rates leveled off.

As the boundaries of acceptable behavior (acceptable, that is, to individuals defending an extended dignity) were gradually redrawn, the gross number of disputes increased, but the rate at which they were taken "to law" diminished. Individuals again knew what to expect and where they stood. The number of unconceded and unresolved claims between strangers always remained higher than between neighbors because, as Christine Heyrman has written, the boundary of acceptable behavior is harder to see when it goes beyond the "town borders."[9]

Public Litigiousness

There was no clear line between public law and private lawsuits in the era of litigiousness. Officeholders could be suitors in their own right, as could the colonial governments. King's attorneys and judges had active private law practices. Although there were rules against peculation—misusing public funds for one's own purposes, taking bribes, and extorting money—officeholders could represent clients who had business contracts from the colony. In short, the modern concept of conflict of interest was not well developed.

What is more, holding more than one office was quite common. The recorder of New York City, its legal adviser, was a prosecutor as well. Some of the incumbents in that office were also legal advisers to the governor, a clear conflict of interest as well as an invitation to chaos. Royal governors sat as judges and chancellors, and other judges held multiple posts. Throughout much of the 1710s, Nicholas Trott of South Carolina was chief judge of the court of common pleas, chief judge of the court of admiralty, and a member of the governor's council. He was not above representing himself and speaking for private clients as well as politicking for his friends, and in his spare time he wrote the first compilation of the colony's laws. Samuel Sewell was simultaneously a judge on Massachusetts' highest court, a justice of the peace and probate judge in his county, and a member of the upper house of the colony. Years later, Thomas Hutchinson of Massachusetts, while performing as the lieutenant governor of the province and sitting in its council, was also the chief justice of its Superior Court of Judicature—and this, like Sewall, with no training in law.

Legal officials were constantly crossing over the boundaries between their many offices and going back and forth between their private law practices and their public duties. Scandals from this constant politicization of the legal process were common. Some of them paralyzed the courts of entire colonies, as when Governor William Cosby of New York, entangled in a bitter conflict with the assembly for back pay, decided to create a wholly new court to hear and decide, among other things, a suit for his own back pay. When this "exchequer court" scam came to nought, he removed his opponent, Lewis Morris, from the supreme court. Only his death three years into his governorship put a stop to his plotting and allowed the courts to return to their business. Morris became governor of New Jersey but did not come away from his spat with Cosby imbued with high public purposes. Instead, Morris tried to use the Jersey courts to further his family's economic interests.

Officials commonly used their authority to persecute their personal enemies in the courts. Nathaniel Byfield was one such partisan, and his story makes fascinating reading. Byfield came to Boston a young man and quickly established himself as a leading merchant in the emerging Anglo-Massachusetts trade network. He would enjoy a long career in law and politics as a representative to the General Court and then as a councillor of the governor. At various times he was also a judge of the court of common pleas and probate for Bristol County and a judge of the vice-admiralty court for the colony. He was a lay judge— he never practiced law, save when he went to court to plead his own cases. One of these ran on for almost two decades and shows the close tie between public office and legal influence in this era of litigiousness.

Byfield was one of the founders of the town of Bristol, gaining from the General Court (in which he then sat) permission to lay out a town and distribute land within its borders. Byfield was not a humble or conciliatory man, and soon he and the other founders of the town were quarreling. The townspeople took sides, local government was in an uproar, and Byfield found himself backed to the wall. A rugged antagonist emerged in Nathaniel Blagrove, owner of the town mill and other property in Bristol. Blagrove was the administrator of the estate of the Hayman family, and in that capacity he brought an action against Byfield for failing to make payments on a mortgage. In fact, Byfield had tried to make good the missed payments, but Blagrove wanted the property, not the payments. The superior court gave judgment to Blagrove. Byfield struck back through the General Court, of which he was currently the Speaker, inducing that assembly to pass an act allowing those owing money on mortgages (including Byfield) to prevent foreclosure by paying what they owed. The act also specified that foreclosure proceedings begun during the previous two years (a period covering the time that Blagrove had filed his suit) were to be retrospectively brought under the new rule. The act did remedy a genuine problem— Massachusetts temporarily had no courts of equity to offer the equity of redemption (preventing foreclosure on mortgages)—but Byfield was not a disinterested do-gooder. Barbara Black, who has traced his twists and turns, ties Byfield's thinking to the issue of dignity and good faith: "From Byfield's perspective, Blagrove's behavior was villainous, an unconscionable attempt to take improper advantage of accidental circumstances [that is, the temporary absence of a court of equity] to impose the full rigor of the common law [which did not allow equity of redemption]."[10]

Byfield was not finished with Blagrove. Byfield not only had "pull" in the General Court; he was also a valuable ally of Governor Joseph Dudley. From the governor he obtained the post of judge of probate (wills and estates) in Bristol County, and then Byfield turned the tables on Blagrove. While sitting as judge in the probate court, Byfield convinced one of the heirs to the Hayman estate to sue Blagrove for mismanagement in the probate court. Brought before Judge Byfield, Blagrove knew he was in trouble. Byfield demanded that Blagrove give a full account of his administration of the entire estate. When Blagrove delayed, Byfield arranged for the governor's son, Paul Dudley, to act as counsel for the heir. At the same time, Byfield himself brought an action against Blagrove for £6,000 in the court of common pleas for not fulfilling his duty to the heir in Byfield's court. Blagrove was being squeezed between Byfield his personal enemy and Byfield the judge. Blagrove tried to appeal to the governor and council, but Governor Dudley, after hearing his son, lawyer Dudley, speak against the appeal, ruled that the common law must take its course without interference from the executive. Blagrove had one hope left: just as a court of equity could allow a defaulting mortgagee to redeem a piece of mortgaged property, it could reduce ("chancer") a penalty bond down to the actual debt owed. Blagrove pleaded that the administration bond of £6,000 was just like a penalty bond, and he should only owe to the heirs what they were promised in the will, a sum considerably smaller than £6,000. Alas, after hearing this argument, the justices of the Superior Court of Judicature, all friends of Byfield, declared that they could not chancer the administration bond because they did not know what the underlying debt was.

The story might have ended here, with Blagrove a crushed victim of highly partisan justice, had Blagrove not been so tenacious. Instead, he resisted paying the £6,000 to the court of probate while he petitioned the General Court to instruct the justices of the superior court to chancer the bond. At last, they agreed and so informed the justices. In effect, the General Court, a legislature, had acted as an appellate court. Now the tables had turned on Byfield. Ordered in his capacity as probate judge to obey the higher court, he refused, and for his refusal (expressed in very intemperate language) he was removed from his post as probate judge.

Byfield v. *Blagrove* demonstrates the way in which personal dignity wove its way into public law as well as private law. It also shows that public officials were not above using their offices for private purposes. If, in the end, the courts did maintain their independence from the other branches of government, the lines between branches and the functions of the branches were not well drawn.

Litigiousness and the Legislature

The litigiousness of public officials created tensions within another part of the legal system: the colonial legislature. With influence peddling rampant, who could stem the tide of suit and countersuit among the ruling class? The answer—in theory—was that the givers of statute law—legislators—could curb corruption among their own number. Reformers in England had challenged Parliament to do as much, though they had little success during Prime Minister Robert Walpole's long tenure. Colonial legislatures might also channel disputes back into the community and away from the courts by making it harder to bring a suit or by passing laws designed to foster alternatives to suit. In fact, the litigation explosion engulfed the givers of law. They became parties to suits themselves. Worse still, the reigning passion for suing began to wreak havoc with the stability and impartiality of the assemblies in which the lawgivers worked.

By the middle of the eighteenth century, colonial legislatures had emerged as fully developed lawmaking bodies. If many colonists were excluded from the franchise, the colonial lower house was still far more representative of colonial opinion than Parliament was of popular opinion in England. Typically, by mid-century the New Jersey assembly was effectively handling six times as many petitions as it handled thirty years before. Colonial legislatures had become increasingly active makers of statute law; the number of laws passed in the Massachusetts General Court increased from seventeen or eighteen at the beginning of the century to thirty-eight each session at the end of the 1750s.[11] These were not so-called "private bills" for the convenience of an individual petitioner but public acts similar to modern legislation. Equally important, the acts were printed and circulated in the colony and served to regulate the inhabitants' behavior far more effectively than the first assemblies' regulatory efforts. For example, throughout the eighteenth century the Pennsylvania assembly had coped with poverty and disease in a far more forthright manner than Parliament had. The Virginia legislature fashioned an intelligent and comprehensive system of quality control for tobacco. In New York and Massachusetts, legislative action had aided the interests of the ports of New York City and Boston and regulated wages and prices in the seagoing industries. As more and more lawyers entered the lower houses in the colonies, statutes became more precise. The lawyers knew how to draft enforceable acts.

These achievements notwithstanding, most colonial legislative sessions were not conducive to reducing the rage for private suits or to finding statutory alternatives to the private lawsuit. The legislatures too often sat as courts themselves to stand above the fray of litigiousness. Private bills, little more than settlements of cases that could have gone to the regular courts, were still passed in the assemblies. A serious deliberative effort by the assemblymen might have curbed the passion for private suits, but as Thomas Jefferson recorded after his first visit to the Maryland assembly in 1766, these bodies were not designed for deliberation:

> The Assembly happens to be sitting at this time . . . in an old courthouse, which judging from it's form and appearance, was built in the year one. I was surprised on approaching it to hear as great a noise and hubbub as you will usually observe at a publick meeting of the planters in Virginia. The first object which struck me after my entrance was the figure of a little old man dressed but indifferently, with a yellow queue wig on, and mounted in the judge's chair. This the gentleman who walked with me informed me was the speaker [of the assembly, that is, the presiding officer]. . . . At one end of the justices' bench stood a man . . . reading a bill then before the house with a schoolboy tone and an abrupt pause at every half dozen words. This I found to be the clerk of the assembly. The mob (for such was their appearance) sat covered [wearing their hats] on the justices and lawyers' benches, and were divided into little clubs amusing themselves in the common chit chat way. I was surprised to see them address the speaker without rising from their seats, and three, four, and five at a time without being checked. . . . In short everything seems to be carried [passed into law] without the house in general's knowing what was proposed.[12]

Jefferson had a point: by the 1760s, the Virginia House of Burgesses was a much more composed and orderly body than the Maryland assembly. Maryland assemblymen indulged their partisanship in divisive roll call votes; Virginia burgesses shunned these public demonstrations of disagreement. The Maryland model was the more common one, however, in the colonial lower houses. In the midst of such noise and confusion, all sorts of ill-considered bills could be passed in the assembly—and were. In 1743, an anti–New York City faction in the New York assembly put together a one-vote majority to pass a bill ending the city's monopoly of ferryboats. Quite naturally commuters to the city resented the monopoly, but the majority did not understand that the ferry tolls were the city's prime source of income. Only the pleas of the city aldermen to the colonial council prevented the city from losing its best revenue producer.

Worse still for any project to diminish individual litigiousness, colonial legislatures had a penchant for indulging in purely partisan exercises, campaigns of intimidation of royal governors, and internal factional struggles. Rudimentary political party organizations radiated out from the assemblies into the electoral districts, wasting the energy and dissipating the precious store of cooperation these bodies needed to confront the most pressing question of mid-century: how to carry on war with the French and the Indians. The vacillation and division of the colonial assemblies in the face of the French and Indian War (1754–63) showed the limits of colonial lawmaking. Assemblies bumbled and stumbled when called upon to raise troops and provide supplies for the war.

Assemblies' power to treat the symptoms of litigiousness in the general population was further undercut by incessant rivalry with the judges. Lower houses in New York and Massachusetts periodically refused to pay judges' salaries and splenetically railed at English authorities who offered to pay the judges out of customs revenues. In New Jersey and Pennsylvania, assemblies and governors spat defiance at each other over the tenure of judges. The governors wanted judges to serve at the pleasure of the crown; lower houses wanted tenure during good behavior or, failing that, at the pleasure of the legislature. Judges of the colonial supreme courts were caught between suspicious assemblies and overbearing governors. In the lower houses, individual litigiousness and political partisanship simply reinforced each other.

Faced with endless bickering, colonial governments joined individual litigants confronting new and complex forms of indebtedness: they all turned to the full-time professional lawyer. The rise of the colonial bar and the substantial law to which this bar gave shape would profoundly and permanently change the relationship between colonial law and people.

CHAPTER FOUR

"Just so th' Unletter'd Blockheads of the *Robe*;

(Than Whom no Greater Monsters on the Globe);

Their Wire-Drawn, Incoherent, Jargon Spin,

Or Lug a Point by Head and Shoulders In"

B y the middle of the eighteenth century, the English colonies in America were maturing. The marks of settlement, clearings and roads, villages and churches, crept inland from the shore and up and down the coast. Within their towns and parishes, the colonists were building—often unknowingly—a more mobile and individualistic world than the one they had left. Lines that divided classes by blood and wealth in the Old World did not disappear in America, but they blurred into multiple overlapping patterns of deference and mobility.

No one's place in society was assured, nor was anyone's wealth safe from catastrophe. In the course of the eighteenth century, some men and women who had risen from indentured servitude to own their own farms slipped back into tenancy. Laborers in Boston and Philadelphia saw their standard of living gradually decline. A few African-Americans were free; many more were debased into chattel slaves. Reduced in numbers by disease and war, American Indians struggled to rebuild communities, often on lands far from home.

Law offered the hope and the semblance of stability in this world of uncertainty and misfortune. Men and women went to law to assert old values and test new ways. Law interceded between disputants and intruded into the everyday lives of towns and parishes. For much of the seventeenth century and into the first decades of the eighteenth century, such law was formal—handed down, in writing, by an authoritative governing body—but not formalistic. It was law that spoke in a tongue ordinary people could understand. In the course of the eighteenth century, that would change. By mid-century, an educated lay person observing a civil suit in the colonial supreme courts would need trained assistance to know what was happening. Law was becoming technical, and increasingly it was the preserve of lawyers.

In counterpoise to the growing sense of Americanness in other areas of life as the eighteenth century progressed, colonial legal exceptionalism was disappearing. As the loosely woven and multicolored patterns of seventeenth-century transmission and reception of law became more orderly and repetitious in the eighteenth century, American law inched toward English law. Local elites to whose influence and leadership many deferred still functioned as officers of the courts in these colonies, but the formative era of American law had ended, and an era of formalization had begun.

The Lawyers

There were lawyers in the first colonies, but the rise of the legal profession to an elite position in America is a story belonging to the eighteenth century. Consumer demand called the legal profession into prominence. At first, the rise of the lawyers was gradual. In sprawling, rural Gloucester County, the heartland of Quaker West Jersey, the original settlers did not need lawyers, and none are mentioned in the first court records. In September 1691, six years after the inhabitants fashioned themselves into a county, John Ithell, surveyor, farmer, and magistrate, "appeared for" John Ireson, the latter sued for trespassing on John Reading's land. Ireson and Reading were actually disputing title to the meadow in question, and given that Reading was the biggest landholder in the new village of Woodbury, Ireson needed help. For it he turned to Ithell, though it did no good. A jury found for Reading. Other parties may have taken Ireson's defeat to heart—three years passed before Richard Whitaker decided he needed counsel in his suit against the trustees of John Willis. Thereafter, counsel was present in a steadily growing minority of cases. More telling, men and women brought to court began to believe they needed counsel. Presented by the grand jury for making off with a neighbor's apple pie, Elizabeth Tomlinson and Edward Eglinton, the latter a notoriously litigious person, convinced the justices that "want of council [counsel]" substantially hurt their ability to defend themselves. The court allowed them time to find an attorney. In 1724, the court clerk even began to docket pending cases by the name of the attorney of record.

Gloucester's first "attorneys" were not trained lawyers at all, but men—and women—of affairs. An attorney was merely a person who represented another person at the bar. On October 6, 1708, John Richards could not be present when his suit against Daniel Lindsey was called. Richards was represented "by his attorney, Susan, his wiff [wife]."[1] Increased litigation in the 1720s and 1730s made lawyering lucrative and attracted able young men, but women were not accepted as apprentices in lawyers' offices, nor were they licensed to practice law by the superior courts. By the 1730s, most of the statutory barriers to law practice for men had fallen, trampled down by throngs of colonists seeking trained assistance in what was fast becoming the American avocation of litigation.

The impetus to hire a lawyer went hand in glove with the increasing complexity and frequency of litigation. The lawyers introduced more formal language, inducing the defendants or plaintiffs who acted for themselves to seek trained help. The lawyers employed the common-law system of pleading, which put a premium on precise and correct formulation of issues, another inducement to hiring legal counsel. Lawyers manipulated special pleading not only to further their clients' interests but also to establish the indispensability of the legal profession. Essential to the emerging formalism of litigation, the lawyers swarmed in the county courts as well as the central courts.

Improvements in the packet service carrying passengers back and forth to England in the same years facilitated the importation of law books and law reports into the colonies. Wealthy lawyers in the colonies were regular clients of English booksellers, often buying works on history and religion as well as technical works on law. By the 1750s, lawyers in every colony had law libraries of considerable size and diversity. Reports of cases and abridgments of the law, along with law dictionaries and form books, were the most popular purchases. The classics remained Edward Coke's *Reports of Cases* (all thirteen volumes) and his *Institutes*, the Statutes at Large of England, Francis Bacon's *Elements of the Common Laws of England*, John Cowell's and Giles Jacob's dictionaries of legal terms, Geoffrey Gilbert's treatises on all manner of legal topics, and numerous abridgments of the laws from Bacon's work in the early seventeenth century to Charles Viner's encyclopedic collection from the mid-eighteenth century.

The law libraries of James Alexander and William Livingston of New Jersey and New York; James Murray, William Smith, Sr., and John Jay of New York; James Gridley and Oxenbridge Thacher of Massachusetts; and John Mercer and George Wythe of Virginia were well stocked with English law books. These men made the practice of law more English even as they began to join in the protest against parliamentary exactions on the colonies.

With the law books came even more lawyers, some trained in the London Inns of Court, others merely solicitors or conveyancers in the mother country seeking to better themselves in the New World. These men brought with them more intimate knowledge and greater familiarity with the common-law system of pleading, itself fueling the drive toward formalization of law.

In every colony by mid-century, young apprentice pleaders stood at the side of older mentors. American lawyers trained themselves by "reading" law as clerks and juniors in established lawyers' chambers or offices. Some of the latter—for example, Joseph Hawley in Massachusetts, William Smith, Sr., in New York, James Alexander in New Jersey, John Dickinson in Pennsylvania, Samuel Chase in Maryland, and George Wythe in Virginia—were sought-after law teachers. Many law students found their apprenticeship intellectually deadening, however. John Adams, for example, slogged through the standard course in English law treatises (most over a century old) before being admitted to practice himself. Although he studied with many of the leading Massachusetts lawyers of his day, he was most struck by an evening with Oxenbridge Thacher. In his *Autobiography* he recalled: "Mr. Thacher, as it was evening when I waited on him, invited me to Tea and then made me smoke Bridgwater tobacco with him, till after ten O Clock. He said nothing about Law, but examined me more severely in Metaphysics. We had Clark and Leibnitz, Descartes, Mal[e]branche and Lock[e], Baxter, Bolin[g]broke and Berk[e]ley, with many others on the Carpet, and Fate, Foreknowledge, Eternity, Immensity, Infinity, Matter and Spirit, Essence and Attribute, Vacuum and Plenum, Space, and Duration, Subjects which neither of Us understood, and which I have long been convinced, will never be intelligible to human Understanding."[2] Adams may have embroidered on the truth—his frustration at the irrelevancy of much of legal education in his day was palpable—but the general thrust of his comments hit the mark.

Adams deplored mindless legal education, but young lawyers like Adams were very professional and had no use for unprofessional conduct and inferior abilities. William Livingston of New York, another brilliant lawyer of Adams' generation, attacked the governors of New York for acting as chancellors of the court of chancery because "very few instances can be assigned of their having been bred to the Profession, or Study of the Law; without a considerable Knowledge of which, it is impossible any man can be qualified for the important Office of a Chancellor."[3] The amateurishness of the colonial high-court judges was a general phenomenon. For example, the Massachusetts Superior Court of Judicature had on its bench from 1720 through 1774 only six men with extensive legal training. True, most of the other twenty-one men who served had some experience as lower court judges, but as the law became more technical, their solid common sense was less appreciated by the trained professional lawyers who practiced law in the court of judicature.

Despite criticism from some quarters, the formalization of the legal profession was a movement that seemed unstoppable. With it came more and more of the external garb—literally wigs and robes in the case of judges—of English legal practice. This "Anglicization" of the law made law practice respectable—it was already lucrative— for the top of the profession at least. In Massachusetts and Virginia, sons of great men studied for the bar. If the quality of legal education did not impress John Adams, it had nevertheless become a requirement for legal practice. Bar associations created by the leading lawyers soon gained the approval of the colonial legislatures, themselves increasingly penetrated by members of the legal profession. Bar examinations went hand in hand with licensing examinations by judges, the result of which was a more influential profession as well as a more English one. With Anglicization it was possible for a coterie of well-educated and well-bred lawyers to attempt to make law practice a preserve of a professional gentry. While these men did not quite succeed in preventing competition from less prominent practitioners, the leaders of the bar did manage to divide the legal profession into jealous factions. The elite of the bar practiced in the central courts, sometimes sat in the legislatures as well, rubbed elbows with the governors and the high-court judges, and looked down on their rural brethren at the county courts as unlearned. The consequences of this condescension were swift and unexpected.

In Virginia, the planter–justices of the peace who dominated the local legal system quickly discovered and greatly resented the attitude of the great lawyers. A struggle for control of the courts, fees, and respectability turned into a matter of honor and disrupted politics at Williamsburg for the rest of the colonial period. Isolated and alienated by the evolving professional legal culture, the justices of the peace resented the sneers of the elite lawyers and their bar associations. Faced with an increasingly technical law and an increasingly sophisticated bar, some justices of the peace depended on their court clerks. A few clerks had formal training (sometimes in England), and at "rules day" before each session of the county court these clerks handled the writs and motions of local lawyers with aplomb and care. Young lawyers could learn a good deal by frequenting clerks' offices on these occasions. Some clerks, like Marmaduke Beckwith of Richmond County, served in their posts for long periods of time, facilitating the flow of information and persons back and forth between a traditional local justice system and the more formal world of law at the capital.

In Massachusetts, untrained local attorneys were crushed by the elite bar. By the 1760s the unlicensed attorneys "could not plead in court on either the county or province level. They were reduced to the lowly function of drafting legal documents and scraping up business for established lawyers."[4] In New York, friction among lawyers and competition for a place at the bar in the various courts were severe. A small group of New York City counselors battled to keep out less well connected lawyers. Elsewhere, lawyers like Daniel Dulany, Jr., a leader of the Maryland bar, routinely scrutinized the lists of newly enrolled lawyers to check for unqualified interlopers. In 1752, he moved to the Prince George's county court that one Abel Pooley be stricken from the list of practitioners because Pooley was a "strolling player." The county court clerk evidently could not tell the difference between a lawyer and an actor—at least not until the actor exceeded the lawyer in indecorous conduct.[5]

Pleading a Lawsuit

Like the colonial courts in which the lawyers practiced, legal procedure varied somewhat from colony to colony. Any short summary of procedure must be a composite. In general, pleading in the colonies in the eighteenth century followed enough of the English model to be recognizable to a lawyer from the mother country, though the precision required of English lawyers was often lost in the colonies through the intervention of lay judges or short-circuited by the inexperience of the American practitioners.

The suit at common law, also called an "action," began with the filing in court of a "writ." In origin, the writ was a document obtained from the king's secretary (his chancellor) which allowed a suitor to bring the action in a royal court. For many years in England, these writs were in Latin and were quite specific. When a plaintiff used the wrong writ to bring the action, the case was dismissed. Writs were returned to the appropriate royal courts during their four terms each year (the courts sat for less than one hundred days each year), a process inviting delay and maximizing paperwork (as well as court costs and legal fees).

The Provisions of Oxford (1258) effectually limited the variety of writs, turning a procedural device into a body of substantive legal rights and wrongs. To deal with situations not covered by the original writs, lawyers and judges developed legal "fictions," thereby protecting the "formulary" or writ-pleading system while allowing the common law to evolve. Fictions allowed parties to try title to land, bring suits into a more convenient court, and avoid cumbersome and outmoded procedural requirements for determination of facts. By the time the Puritans began their campaign to reform pleading in the seventeenth century, common-law procedure was littered with fictions, evidence of the piecemeal advance of the law and stumbling blocks to more thorough reform.

The purpose of common-law writ pleading in the colonies was to reduce the legal issue to a single "cause of action" and confine juries to deciding a narrowly defined factual question. Abstract general concepts such as "contract," "tort," and "property," which became the basis of law teaching and litigation at the end of the nineteenth century, had no place in eighteenth-century common-law pleading. The critical first step in bringing a common-law suit was thus the choice of the appropriate writ.

Once the original writ was filed, the colonial court informed the defendant that litigation had begun and summoned the defendant to appear. In court, plaintiff's declaration laid out one version of the facts. Defendants had to answer the declaration. They might confess judgment; there the action ended and payment of damages and costs was arranged. They might deny all the facts (plead "the general issue"), assert facts excusing them (plead "in bar of the action"), challenge the technical correctness of the writ on which the action was brought (plead "abatement on the writ"), or admit that some or all of the factual allegations in the declaration were true but insist that they were not sufficient to sustain the particular action brought by the plaintiff (plead "special" or "general" demurrer). The plea in abatement and the demurrer were not matters for a jury, and one was not impaneled to hear the dispute over such pleas.

The defendant's reply was not confined to the version of the facts presented in the writ but was limited to the underlying transaction or event that brought the plaintiff to court. If the plaintiff alleged that the defendant owed him or her money, and defendant wanted to reply that he or she was owed money by the plaintiff in some other matter (a "set off"), or that a third party was responsible for the damage done ("joinder" of another party), the defendant had to bring a separate action into the courts as a plaintiff or go into the courts of equity and seek relief there.

Back and forth the pleas went, through a course of "replications," "rebutters," "rejoinders," and "surrebutters." If plaintiffs failed to appear in a colonial trial court, they were "non-suited." If defendants failed to answer or appear, they were held in "default" and had to pay the judgment plus the court costs. Meanwhile, in order to ensure that defendants did not disappear or squirrel away their property, plaintiffs could obtain a variety of intermediate writs to attach defendants' property or arrest their flight. Defendants jailed by the sheriff were ordinarily freed on bail or given the right to move freely about the jailhouse and its environs.

Most suits did not go to trial. They were settled "in the shadow of the courthouse" by negotiation, confession and payment, or arbitration of some sort. At trial, the evidence offered was primarily documentary. Witnesses could be called and examined on oath, but the testimony of persons who had any monetary interest in the suit was barred. The dispute rested upon a very narrow base of controverted facts, and there was little cross-examination of witnesses. The jury was expected to reach its verdict upon its independent assessment of evidence, not upon its judgment about who was telling the truth and who was lying.

After the trial verdict, judicial order, or default was entered, another, final series of writs, paid for by the parties, started the "execution" of judgment. Sometimes a successful plaintiff had to pay for many rounds of writs before the sheriff found the defendant and obtained the damages or took possession of the defendant's land and chattels and sold these at auction to pay off the plaintiff.

Some able and spirited colonial lawyers railed that the system of pleading was needlessly complex and often hindered the court from coming to the merits of the case. William Livingston caricatured the pleading system in poetry:

> Suppose a Limner figur'd in a Piece,
> A Horse's Body with a human Face:
> Above a Virgin, beautiful and hale,
> But shap'd beneath into a Fish's Tail;
> At last, in varied Plumage drest the Whole,
> Wou'd you not laugh, and brand him a Fool?
> Just so th' unletter'd Blockheads of the *Robe* [the lawyers]
> (Than whom no greater Monsters on the Globe)
> Their wire-drawn, incoherent, Jargon spin,
> Or lug a Point by head and shoulders in.[6]

A few years later, young Alexander Hamilton of New York, in the midst of his training for the bar, ruefully remarked that "the Court . . .

lately acquired . . . some faint Idea that the End of Suits at Law is to investigate the Merits of the Cause, and not to entangle [lawyers and their clients] in the Nets of technical terms."[7]

Substantive Law

As procedure varied from colony to colony, so did "substantive" law, the rules and precedents that determined the outcome of disputes. One should bear in mind the fact that in colonial law no sharp boundary separated procedure from substance—a writ, for example, was both a procedural device and a substantive claim. As with procedure, one can create a composite picture of colonial substantive law. In overall content, colonial substantive law was English law, but there were differences, and these are almost as important as the similarities.

REAL ESTATE

The common lawyers had liberated much of English real estate and inheritance practice from the dead hand of feudalism by 1607, but some of the king's friends who were granted proprietorships in the colonies wanted to reestablish feudalism. The seven noble proprietors of the Carolinas, for example, believed that they could send their estate managers and servants to America and rule in the style of medieval barons. In New York, leading Dutch and English families pried great swaths of land from the government and yearned for the privileges of lords of the manor. The feudal dreams of these men vanished when they came face to face with the labor shortage in the colonies. Even when colonial magnates and "river gods" could find men and women to till the soil, there was so much land that no free person need bind himself or herself to serve another for life. As the governor of New York reported in 1700, "what man, will be such a fool to become a base tenant . . . [on such manors in New York] when for crossing Hudson's River that man can for a song purchase a good freehold in the Jerseys?"[8] In Virginia, indentured servants whose labor contracts required that they work for their masters for a term of years knew that the end of service would bring them ownership of a small farmstead. The sprawling Hudson River estates of the Livingstons, Van Cortlandts, and Philipses depended upon contractual labor—tenants whose leases were negotiated, not imposed. So, too, in Pennsylvania, the many tenants on the proprietors' lands parlayed multiyear leases into concessions and privileges.

By the seventeenth century, the common law allowed most English men to freely alienate their lands, and statutes provided for the transfer of property, both movable personal goods (chattels) and real estate, through wills. English law had not stood still. Nevertheless, American ways of distributing land had run ahead of significant reforms in English practice. If the English no longer actually required "turf and twig," actual delivery of possession, for the transfer of land, English law was still a patchwork of newer rules and older requirements. Some of the latter came to America as customs, not law. For example, Virginia vestrymen were required to "procession" the survey lines in the parish and report their findings much as men of the medieval English parish "beat the bounds" of the parish, but the right to land in Virginia was not based upon medieval tenures.

Early in the course of settlement, the colonists opted for a clean, straightforward approach to the transfer of title to lands. Almost all the colonies adopted the "deed" and "record" system. In deed and record, title passed with the exchange of a deed, a memorandum of sale. The deed was then recorded in a county or colonial record book. The title was fully secure only with the record (a prior deed lost out to a later deed that had been recorded first). The deed described the property, giving its boundaries and extent. Subsequent sellers merely endorsed the deed to new buyers; the latter bore the burden of recording the transaction. Some of the deeds ran to many pages; others were quite short. Some mentioned a duty to pay quitrents to the king or his agents; others did not. In the end, it was almost impossible for anyone to collect quitrent for the crown. Behind the introduction of easier, cheaper, and more egalitarian ways to buy and sell land was a decision to exploit the vast expanse of land adopted by colonial governments: "All in all, it was easier to use land as a cheap, convenient subsidy [to attract people] than as a means to fetter a restless population."[9]

Despite the availability of land and the ease with which it could be bought and sold, possession of land was not evenly distributed among the settlers. True, in New York, Virginia, and elsewhere a "headright" system linked 40- and 50-acre parcels of land to immigration, but this land was given to the agent who arranged for the passage of the immigrant. Many land-hungry immigrants ultimately took possession of these parcels—provided they survived the ocean crossing and years of toil in the colonies—but most land grants by the colonial and imperial governments acceded to a different version of land hunger. Land was used as payment for political support, and hundreds of thousands of acres in the colonies were tied up in this way.

In New York and New Jersey, legal title to these enormous tracts of land was bitterly and endlessly contested in the courts. Insofar as the original grants were the fruit of political deals, one governor's reward to his friends, a new governor felt free to try to grab back the lands and give them to his own supporters. New York politics was convulsed by this revolving-door policy of large land grants, and the courts were politicized in the process. In New Jersey, grantees of the first Quaker proprietors, purchasers of Indian titles, and recipients of later royal largess butted heads in court and threatened one another in the streets. Courts in all the colonies became political arenas when political factions sought to test one another's control of land.

Throughout the colonies, powerful families gained control of vast tracts. Such grants of land were farmed as great estates with servants, subdivided and leased out to tenants, resold as speculative ventures, or kept in reserve for later generations of the family. Land speculation would remain a leading industry and the ruling mania of the founders of the American republic. Speculation sometimes fostered the rapid if largely undirected exploitation of the fields and forests; on other occasions it acted like a drug and left its addicts in debtors prisons. Patentees had to fend off squatters, of course, sometimes by pitting squatter against squatter. In colonial Maine, "settlers and proprietors 'negotiated' their conflicting interests in a succession of petty confrontations. Through a shifting array of tactics—possession fences, fair promises, dire threats, petitions to authorities, ritual repossessions, cabin burnings, and lawsuits—men took the measure of one another's power."[10] Deeds conferred a right to claim property in land; actual possession was another matter entirely.

INHERITANCE

In 1540, Parliament allowed testators (men and women who made wills) to devise their land to whom they pleased under certain restrictions. With a few regional exceptions, when there was no will (when the landowner died "intestate"), all real estate passed to the eldest son. This was "primogeniture." If the family claimed rights as freeholders or copyholders in a manor under a lord, and the owner died without a will, the "custom of the country" determined the distribution of land. Almost all of England customarily required "impartible" inheritance— the eldest son once again got all. The county of Kent in the southeast of England allowed for "partible" inheritance, a more equal division of land among the male children.

Chattels were distributed in England according to a wholly different system than that used for land when the owner died intestate. Such distribution had been the preserve of church courts, and the Statute of

Distribution of 1670 adopted formulas developed by the church. Wives got one-third; the rest was divided among the children. If no children survived, the wife divided the chattels with the nearest male relatives.

In the colonies as in England, inheritance law was partly statutory, partly based upon judicial precedents. Many of the colonies created probate courts (in New York the "prerogative court") or devoted separate portions of the superior courts' sessions to hear and approve the provisions of wills. Commissioners were appointed to take an inventory of the estate if one was not included in the will. These inventories have allowed social historians to study the accumulation and distribution of property.

Insofar as the law permitted men and women to make wills, the actual dispersement of family property varied according to the desires of individuals. Wills reflected family strategies for building funds of capital or disbursing accumulated wealth, sometimes concentrating the wealth in a few hands, more often distributing it among surviving spouse and children. In Bucks County, Pennsylvania, for example, testators tended to give equal shares to all their sons but favored sons over daughters. In the South, testators generally treated their sons equally and left nearly equal portions of their estates to their daughters, albeit tying the latter up in life estates or irrevocable trusts rather than allowing the daughter (and lurking behind her, the son-in-law) to own the property. In North and South, the equality women enjoyed in distributions of property and assignments as the executors of estates disappeared by the mid-eighteenth century. The reason was simple—in the first years of settlement there were very few women, a fact inflating their importance, and surviving sons were likely to be too young to act as executors of their late fathers' estates. In later years the sex ratio approached one to one, women lost much of their bargaining power, and sons were likely to live long enough to act as executors of the family estate.

Many colonists wrote wills. So often did New Englanders use these legal instruments that one scholar has used signatures on them as a proxy for literacy in the region. The colonial will was similar in form from Maine to the sea islands of South Carolina. Nuncupative (oral) wills were evidently not common. Some parents did not wait for their own death to divide the family real estate and personal valuables among children. Pre-testamentary gifts to grown children were very common in New England. The gifts allowed children to marry, farm the land, and begin to have their own children without fear of want.

In the South as in New England, parental, that is, paternal, control of property was used to control the conduct of children. If equal shares were the rule (though the son who stayed in the family home to take care of his parents in their dotage was likely to fare better than his siblings), sons and daughters often had to wait until they married, or until their father retired or died, to receive their portion. The distribution of the wealth of a family from one generation to the next, sometimes called "family capitalism," has been variously conceived by scholars as a device to advance in a market economy or a traditional means to protect a family line. The mentality of the giver or the testator must be inferred from the gift and the will, not easy for the historian to do.

The use of wills to control children, denying them autonomy but promising them an equal distribution of property if they contributed their labor to the family enterprise, had unanticipated consequences in coastal New England. As land deteriorated in quality and families divided it into ever-smaller parcels with each generation of offspring, children of the fourth and fifth generations not only faced the unpleasant prospect of getting no land, they also saw with poignant clarity that their status in the towns could never equal that of their forebears. Purchase Brown of Concord came from a leading family in the town, but in the 1750s his prospects were dim if he stayed at home. His grandfather had left a farmstead of 100 acres, but Purchase was one of a dozen children of David Brown, and the appraisers of the estate had warned his father against splitting it further. "Purchase could not progress gradually from working his father's farm to running his own nearby, nor could he count on spending all his days in the same familiar surroundings. . . . [although] By delaying marriage, boarding at his father's house, and hiring out as a laborer, he might eventually, if he scrimped and saved, acquire a small farm of his own."[11] The store of family capital was exhausted by many generations of children. Men and women facing Purchase Brown's situation would soon be found in the mills and factories of New England at the looms or the cobbler's bench, or leading their families to new farmland in the West.

When there was no will, widows of intestates retained possession for life of one-third of the land and one-third of the chattels. In New England, statutes provided for partible inheritance, a double share—the biblical portion—to the oldest son. In the middle and southern colonies, the custom of primogeniture was retained from England, the oldest son getting all of the land, though he had to settle for an equal share of the chattels with his brothers and sisters.

The New England intestacy statutes directly confuted the English law of primogeniture, leaving the heirs open to a legal attack from the oldest son, or the oldest male in a collateral line if the intestate had no sons. The charters of the colonies barred colonial statutes from violating English law. The Connecticut and Massachusetts intestacy laws were challenged in *Winthrop v. Lechmere* (Connecticut, 1728) and *Phillips v. Savage* (Massachusetts, 1733). The first case involved two of the greatest families in the colony and a very large parcel of real estate. The Connecticut General Court upheld the colonial statute, but after nearly a decade of fumbling the Privy Council advised the king to disallow the statute. Despite this ruling, the Connecticut authorities apparently continued to act as though the statute were still in force. In the Massachusetts case, the colonial courts upheld the statute, and after Massachusetts' agents waged a spirited defense of the colonial statute, the Privy Council went along with the colony. In effect the Privy Council had conceded the existence of an American law of intestacy sanctioned by long usage, although it cited as its reason the crown's approval of the statute in 1695.

Women fared less well than men under American inheritance practices. Daughters received smaller shares than sons under the laws of intestacy and usually fared even worse when there was a will than they would have had the parent died intestate. American courts continued to regard a married woman as "feme covert" whose legal rights and property were totally merged with her husband's. The wife could not sell off property without her husband's consent, nor could she bind herself by contract. Her husband had the right to sell off any or all of the couple's property without the consent of his wife, even if the property was brought into the marriage by her, though there were qualifications upon this sort of sale. Husbands could not sell property the wife inherited, and if she appeared to consent to such a sale, she would be privately examined about her true feelings by a magistrate. Some colonial courts would enforce premarital agreements under which women could protect their own property against coverture. These agreements often involved the creation of a "trust" into which brides-to-be put their property. Southern courts tended to be more solicitous of these agreements than northern courts, and southern chancellors protected trust funds from the husbands' creditors. So, too, southern chancellors insisted that the widow keep her dower (the one-third lifetime interest in the marriage's real estate) against all claims. Indeed, southern courts assured widows a one-third portion of the personal property as well, enabling women to retain household goods and personal articles of value.

Behind what seemed to be small steps toward equality of the sexes under the law of inheritance was a lingering and pervasive commitment to a paternalistic society and a paternally dominated domestic sphere. If affection and companionship were becoming more common in marriage and child rearing in the eighteenth century than had been true before, married women's property law was not intended to liberate women. Susan Staves argues persuasively that in England over these same years "when individual husbands accumulate[d] sufficient property to make a forced share [i.e., dower] significantly more than subsistence for a woman of that rank, then forced share schemes [were] evaded or repealed. . . . In male-dominated society, rules concerning married women's property have always functioned to facilitate the transmission of significant property from male to male; entitlements to women have been to provide them with subsistence for themselves and minor children dependent upon them."[12] A similar argument may be made for the colonies.

Non-English immigrants were sometimes scandalized by the English rules of intestacy. In Germany (as in the New England towns) communal farming and local custom had led to the continual division of family lots into smaller portions, but Germans coming to the southern colonies viewed with distaste the rules of primogeniture. They were accustomed to Roman law of community property in marriage and equal division of property at the death of one of the spouses. In the northern colonies, principally Pennsylvania, German newcomers objected to intestacy laws that favored the eldest son. Leaders of the German community urged all German men and women to leave wills to secure their own arrangements for their children's portions. These included provisions for the surviving spouse to retain what he or she had brought into the marriage; the rest was ordinarily partitioned equally among surviving relatives. The will itself became a way in which Germans could control the distribution of family property according to distinctive elements of German cultural inheritance, safe from the foreignness of English and American inheritance law.

MARRIAGE AND DIVORCE

Colonial marriage and divorce law was slightly more open to the needs of a mobile, heterogeneous, opportunistic, fluid society than English marriage and divorce law. In America, as in England before the Marriage Act of 1753, a man and a woman could enter into marriage by mutual consent and open cohabitation. No formal steps were necessary, though many couples did engage in religious ceremonies.

Ending the marriage was much more difficult. England, though a Protestant nation, retained a Roman Catholic view of divorce—there was none. The church courts could annul marriages for cause (impotence, affinity, consanguinity) or allow separation on condition that the partners remained celibate until one or the other died. In 1670, Lord de Roos was able to obtain permission from the House of Lords to remarry after he proved his wife guilty of adultery. In effect, the Lords had granted him a legislative divorce. After de Roos's successful plea, legislative bills of divorce were theoretically available, but there were still very few legislative divorces in England—only ninety between 1692 and 1785—and they cost more than a poor person could afford.

Divorce was easier and more frequent in many of the colonies. New England Puritans regarded marriage not as a sacrament but as a contract, which misconduct by either partner might breach. The Massachusetts General Court and later the governor and his council simply took upon themselves the power to grant a divorce on grounds of adultery of either partner, as well as cruelty or desertion. Puritan authorities made every effort to effect a reconciliation, but when those efforts failed, they decreed the divorce. There was no statute authorizing this course, merely a disposition on the part of the government to grant the divorce upon petition of one of the parties.

Couples did not rush to the General Court to get divorces. In Massachusetts and in Connecticut, whose divorce practices were even more liberal than those of Massachusetts, there was rarely one petition per year in the seventeenth century. In the next century, the number of petitions steadily increased. Between 1692 and 1785, the Massachusetts General Court heard 229 petitions for divorce, 101 of them from men, and granted 143. The Connecticut Superior Court would grant almost 1,000 divorces before 1800. The assemblies of Rhode Island and New Hampshire also severed marriages upon petition of one of the spouses and a finding of adultery or, more commonly, desertion. Early in the century men were more successful at getting divorces than women, but at the end of the colonial era, as more and more cases came to the court, women began to gain divorce as easily as men. It may be that "the equalization of the consequences of adultery by either spouse, which was unmistakably the reason for the increasing success of women petitioners . . . signified a retreat from hierarchical models and an advance toward ideals of complimentality in the prevailing conception of the marriage relationship,"[13] but even those New England women successful in severing the bonds of matrimony faced the prospect of public shame.

New York and Pennsylvania allowed divorces, but only for adultery. In what at first blush appears an odd reversal of regional preferences one sees in protection of the property rights of women, southern courts and legislatures refused to liberalize divorce, allowing only annulments and celibate separations. The answer to the puzzle may be that southern courts secured women's property against creditors of their husbands not to inaugurate an era of feminism, but to protect great families' wealth—and the plantation system on which such accumulations relied—against dissipation. This impulse did not lend itself to facilitating the breakdown of families, particularly early in the period of settlement, when women were so scarce and therefore so valuable as marriage partners. One could obtain legislative bills of divorce when one partner had disappeared (again, perhaps, to protect the emergence of a planting elite), though these were sometimes disallowed by the Privy Council in England. In all, divorce law in America was different from that in England, and in some clear cases more liberal.

CHURCH AND STATE

Although similar to Roman Catholicism in precept, English divorce law rested not upon Roman law but upon English church law. When a church was "established" in a country as in England—that is, when there was an official, state-sponsored religion—church courts enforced a broad range of religious regulations running from sexual good conduct to conformity in worship. After the Reformation in England, Parliament assigned many of these judicial functions to the civil courts, but the close tie between church and state continued to dictate public enforcement of private morality. What is more, the law demanded conformity of worship, for the lawmakers feared that toleration of religious differences would undermine allegiance to the crown. Europe in the seventeenth century was bitterly divided along religious lines. The treaty that ended the Thirty Years' War in Germany (1618–48) made the religion of the prince the religion of his state, for no practical prince could afford to ignore the political consequences of religious dissent.

The nature of settlement in the colonies undercut but did not undo the relationship between civil and religious authority. The Puritans no sooner fled the persecution of the high church in England than they restated the ideal of religious uniformity in their new home. Indeed, initially they saw themselves as a model for the reformation of the English Protestant church—a conceit they had to surrender when they refused to return to England to aid their brethren in the Civil War. Although Puritan ministers had no power to punish religious dissenters, the magistrates did. Sectaries such as Anne Hutchinson and Roger Williams were driven out of Massachusetts for daring to question the authority of the magistrates in matters of conscience. The magistrates in the colony of New Haven were even more rigorous in ferreting out dissent. Maryland, a colonial haven for Catholics persecuted in England, was rent by religious factionalism when Puritans from England and New England arrived. Rhode Island, a safe harbor for Puritans driven out of Massachusetts, adopted a policy of official toleration—of Protestants only. This concession led not to harmony, but to campaigns by Baptists for full religious freedom. Connecticut attempted to achieve harmony by instituting synods of elders—in effect switching from the Massachusetts plan of Congregationalism to a form of Presbyterianism. The result was not uniformity but conflict over the proper form of church governance. After 1701, the Anglican "Society for the Propagation of the Gospel in Foreign Parts," a missionary effort directed by the bishop of London to Christianize the Indians, entered the New England colonies. Little was done for (or against) the Indians by the Anglican ministers, but they quickly set up shop in Boston and New Haven to try to convert Puritans back to Episcopacy. Pennsylvania was more tolerant of religious dissent than any New England colony, which ironically fostered splits among the Quakers. Civil authorities in the colonies, hard put to protect the settlers against Indian and European raiders, weakened by disputes over colonial autonomy with English authorities, and underfunded and understaffed from top to bottom, simply could not insist on strict conformity to any established church.

The very mixed state of the ministry in the southern churches, where Anglican worship was theoretically established—some ministers were able and well born, others were not so respectable or competent—did nothing to amend this unofficial but pervasive religious pluralism. In Virginia and South Carolina, Anglican ministers were often ill paid. Vestrymen, chosen for their status in the community rather than their piety, were supposed to ensure that the churches and the churchmen were well kept. Instead, they often quarreled with their ministers over salaries. Some of these quarrels ended in the civil courts, where the juries joined with the vestrymen against the ministers instead of supporting the established church.

The advent of the Great Awakening in 1739, the first of many American revival movements, shattered the hopes of some sectarians that their religion would become orthodoxy throughout the colonies. Visiting Anglican preachers like George Whitefield and native Puritan enthusiasts such as Jonathan Edwards and James Davenport led revivals in churches and in fields, dividing Congregationalists into New

Lights and Old Lights, and Presbyterians into New Siders and Old Siders. Using many of the same methods, Baptist and Methodist preachers gained converts.

In the old towns of New England, factions within congregations flew at one another, ministers were hastily hired and ignominiously fired, and new churches formed according to the worshipers' choice of minister. In the backwoods of Virginia, the authority of the Anglican parish swayed in the wind of Methodist and Baptist preaching, the latter sometimes sweeping up slaves in its enthusiasm and lack of pretention. The statutes governing tithing, the choice and authority of ministers, and regulation of immorality remained on the books but in practice were often ignored. Religious affiliation became a matter of individual volition. Perhaps even more important, the preaching of the evangelicals created a new language of egalitarianism. Grace could now be found in the human heart, and the gates of heaven were opened to all who sincerely wished to enter. The same language, in a political context, would infuse popular protest in the 1770s.

CRIMINAL LAW

Like the law of religious observance, criminal law was public law. It rested primarily upon statutes, promoted well-defined public policy aims, and fell equally upon all classes—at least in theory. Were one to reexamine the roots of the "pleas of the crown," the crimes for which a person would be prosecuted in the king's courts of early England, however, one would find that public policy was closely tied to the interests of the king and the elite in society and that the criminal law did not apply equally to all manner of persons. Criminal law in the colonies was not quite so conscious of the status of the accused and the accuser, but as in England, colonial criminal law enforcement did reflect social and economic rank.

When the medieval kings of England began to extend their criminal jurisdiction, their purpose was to protect the crown against subversion. Royal criminal law responded to direct attacks upon the security of the king. Treason and "murder" (the killing of Normans by Saxons from ambush) were the first crimes in which the crown took an interest, and these were punishable by death. They were called felonies and were gradually distinguished from less serious offenses or "misdemeanors." Trial of felonies in the royal courts—first by combat or ordeal, later by jury—replaced family feuds and personal vengeance. In feudal England, status mattered. Noble offenders could even buy a pardon in advance of trial. By the sixteenth century, when religious conflict replaced civil war among the nobles as the chief danger to the state, refusal to attend the services of the Church of England was added to the list of felonies. In the later years of the seventeenth century, with increasing commercialization of the English economy, legislative acts underwriting new forms of enterprise or creating new mediums of exchange included provision for severe punishment of those who destroyed the new form of property or endangered the new kind of enterprise. By the middle of the eighteenth century, destruction of industrial and agricultural machinery had become capital offenses.

In England, the means for easing the severity of felony law also served reasons of state. "Benefit of clergy," transportation, and pardon were purely discretionary mitigations of penalty. Punishment for a host of capital offenses was mitigated when the defendant pleaded benefit of clergy, that is, the defendant averred that he was a man of the cloth. He proved his claim by reading a verse from the Bible, usually the Fifty-first Psalm (sometimes referred to as the "neck verse" because its recital saved the defendant from hanging). In its original form benefit of clergy was limited to priests and those in religious orders. By allowing this exception to the rigor of its laws, the crown offered a valuable privilege to the church. By the middle of the eighteenth century, benefit of clergy was available for many offenses and could be pleaded by lay men and women as well as clerics.

In the eighteenth century, English felony law was also mitigated by "transportation" of convicts for terms of seven or fourteen years. Transportees were sent to the colonies, under guard, and placed with masters who needed and paid for the convicts' labor. Some of these convicts were men and women whom the crown was glad to send away from England for political reasons; others were poor farm laborers who had engaged in some form of protest against their working conditions—for example, by wrecking agricultural machinery or setting crops on fire. A good many transportees were simply professional criminals.

The king, upon the request of the home secretary and with the approval of the trial judge, issued pardons to more than 50 percent of those convicted of capital offenses. Such pardon was purely discretionary, a free gift of the king's grace. Its use reaffirmed his authority and his mercy; the promise of it could be used to turn offenders into informers; the threat of its refusal hung over every unrepentant defendant. Succor from above reminded the convict and the potential wrongdoer that criminal law and courts were the agencies of the state.

The community could interpose itself between this regime of criminal justice and defendants brought to trial. The victims of crime often came from the same class as the offenders, lived in the community, and took an interest in criminal law enforcement. Victims, jurors, and judges wanted order and public safety, but they understood that some crimes were the direct results of poverty and want. Juries regularly mitigated the severity of the laws. When the defendant was a first offender—for example, a child accused of grand larceny (felonious theft)—juries almost always reduced the value of the object taken to less than 12 pence, turning the offense into petty larceny and saving the child from the hangman. Judges went along with this common subterfuge.

Colonial criminal law followed the contours of but was never as severe as English criminal law. In the early colonies, labor was always scarce and thus greatly valued. No colony ever duplicated the severity of punishment for crime on the English statute books, for no colony could afford to lose any of its laborers. Some colonists, notably the Puritans and the Quakers, remembered how vigorously and unfairly the criminal law had been used against them in England. In early New England, burglary and robbery were not capital offenses unless the defendant was a repeater. Grand larceny was never capital. In the first Quaker colonies, the death penalty was reserved for murder. Other serious offenses were punished by triple restitution to the victim (the biblical formula) or hard labor.

In the South, whose criminal codes more closely resembled England's than did those of the northern colonies, and whose concern for status of offender and victim more closely paralleled the mother country's, the criminal law still never duplicated the severity of England's. The greatest difference was in the game laws. In England, poaching in the king's royal forest preserves or upon the lands of noblemen—indeed, carrying firearms when not training with the militia—was a serious offense for commoners. Repeaters could expect a death sentence. Free colonial men and women could carry weapons, and freemen in almost all the colonies were expected to take part in militia exercises. There were no laws against hunting in the forests. In the South, where open fields and hunting became ways of life, game laws would have been unthinkable.

On occasion, colonial criminal law would appear savage to modern sensibilities. Men were executed for bestiality and buggery, and women were whipped for bearing bastards. In these areas colonial law and practice was in perfect accord with the mother country. Witchcraft was punishable by death in England as in the colonies. Despite the many prosecutions in Massachusetts and Connecticut, there was nothing uniquely Puritan about punishment of witchcraft.

Colonial criminal law moved closer to English criminal law in the eighteenth century, particularly in Massachusetts and Pennsylvania. Indeed, the 1690s and 1700s were a watershed in the criminal law in many of the colonies—an end of an era of leniency in punishment of crimes against property. In part this was one more example of the Anglicization of the colonial law. In part the new stringency of colonial laws against larcenies betrayed lawmakers' growing apprehensions that maldistribution of wealth and scarcity of opportunity among the poorer working classes in the colonies would lead to an increase in crime. If the initial reluctance of colonial lawmakers to authorize capital punishment reflected the great value placed on labor in the early colonies, as the labor scarcity diminished, the reason for leniency disappeared. During the revolutionary era, another rationale for reform of the criminal law took hold, a belief in the basic goodness of people and the reformatory capacity of institutions. The result was the introduction of the "penitentiary," an asylum where criminals could be induced to change themselves into productive republican citizens.

English and colonial courts not only heard charges of serious crimes. Far more common were misdemeanors, such as assault, battery, sexual and religious misconduct, and other lesser offenses. Grand juries "presented" information about these offenses to the court, or the magistrates and sheriffs gave "information" about them to the judges. The presentments had a strong gender bias. Women were prosecuted for fornication and bearing bastard children far more often than men, despite the fact that men had a hand in these activities. In Connecticut, single women were tried for the offense five times more often than men. "For single women the experience of being haled into court on the criminal charge of fornication entailed a sharp sense of self-abasement, personal embarrassment, and responsibility for bringing shame on one's family."[14] Men were presented for drunkenness and fighting far more often than women in all the colonies.

Over time, the interests of grand juries changed, resulting in shifting patterns of presentments. For example, as Gwenda Morgan demonstrated, Richmond County, Virginia, grand jurors presented their neighbors for not attending church far more often at the beginning of the eighteenth century than at the end of the colonial period. The grand jurors' concern for sexual immorality peaked in the 1720s and then faded. Explanations for these variations must be speculative, but one may posit that new statutes shifting the burden for ensuring that Virginians went to church from the vestrymen to the county court may account for the surge in grand jury presentments for that offense at the beginning of the century. So, too, the rise in premarital pregnancies that Edward Shorter, Daniel Scott Smith, and Michael Hindus documented for the first half of the eighteenth century may have come to the Old Dominion and outraged the grand jurors until a new generation of planters became accustomed to the phenomenon.

Defendants in these cases confessed or were convicted far more often than defendants accused of serious crimes. For example, early in the century Delaware Valley defendants either submitted to the court or were pronounced guilty more than 90 percent of the time, a typical outcome in misdemeanors. The punishment for these crimes included fines, pillory, and sometimes whipping. Most often, the court ordered the defendant to post a bond for future good behavior. The defendant ordinarily had to find "sureties," other members of the community, to join the defendant in posting the bond. These bonds were forfeit if the defendant went back to his or her old ways, in effect turning the sureties into probation officers, else they would lose their bond money.

CRIMINAL PROCEDURE, TRIAL, AND
REPRESENTATION BY LEGAL COUNSEL

In assessing the extent and direction of procedural rights it is difficult not to indulge modern prejudices. Our criminal justice system, following the Supreme Court's interpretations of the Bill of Rights and the Fourteenth Amendment, is far more solicitous of the procedural rights of the accused than could have been imagined in seventeenth- or eighteenth-century England or America. The resulting tendency is to lose sight of the objectives of early modern criminal procedure and substitute modern ideals. One then looks for and magnifies evidence of the origins of these procedural guarantees—the historical fallacy of presentism.

True, the seventeenth century criminal trial in England and America was changing in its contours from an order-keeping device to a test of individual guilt or innocence, and with that shift came greater concern for improved fact-finding. From what was, too often, little more than an argument between the accused and their accusers in front of a judge and a jury, the criminal trial was moving toward the adversarial cut and thrust of its modern descendant. Nevertheless, formal protection for the defendant was in its infancy.

In England and its colonies, when a serious crime was discovered, the justice of the peace examined witnesses and obtained evidence. He could detain suspects for questioning and decide whether to allow them bail or hold them in custody. Defendants might languish in jail for weeks or months before the court convened, but once the court was ready, procedure moved swiftly. Defendants had to be indicted by a grand jury before they could be brought to trial. The grand jury rarely spent much time deciding if it endorsed the prosecution or found that it had no merit. Trial followed.

The community turned out to observe criminal trials for serious offenses. Curiosity played a part, as did concern for the victim of the crime or the defendant. Criminal trials were also markers of what a community would and would not tolerate from its members. By gathering at the trial, the community gave visible testimony to its shared values. In this context, the physical arrangements at trial were almost as important as the words of law. The judges sat in their majesty at a raised bench. The jurors sat by themselves on benches surrounded by a wooden railing. They represented the community (indeed, the law required that they be resident in the "vicinage"). Suspects had already been separated from the community, friends, and family. Often as not, they had spent weeks or months in jail. Their appearance and health had suffered. Brought into the courtroom to stand alone in a raised box away from any who could aid and comfort, they already appeared different, deviant, and dangerous before the first words of the indictment were spoken.

In Elizabethan and Stuart England, criminal trial had been a straightforward matter. The defendant's life and limb depended upon convincing a judge and jury that he or she was not guilty. According to Sir Thomas Smith, a lawyer and lay churchman who advised Queen Elizabeth on the law, when the judge had finished questioning the witnesses and the accused in the presence of the jury, he was to tell the jury, "Good men (saith he) ye of the enquest, ye have heard what these men say against the prisoner, you have also heard what the prisoner can say for himselfe, have an eye to your oathe, and to your dutie, and doe that which God shall put in your mindes to the discharge of your consciences, and marke well what is said."[15] The jury returned its verdict, often without retiring, and always without "meat nor drinke nor fire," on case after case. James Cockburn has estimated that 40 percent of all those indicted were acquitted.[16] Combined with the number of defendants whom grand juries refused to indict, a much more difficult figure to estimate, we might conclude that more than two-thirds of those individuals bound over for criminal trial were set free. Clearly the community—the jurors—played a vital, sometimes a controlling, role in English criminal justice.

The records of eighteenth-century London and Surrey courts tell a different story of trial, one closer to our own experience. In the 1730s new players strode upon the trial stage—counsel for the prosecution and defense. The lawyers never appeared in more than a small portion of the total number of cases, no more than 20 percent, but in their cut and thrust with one another, their colloquies with the judges, and their caustic, sometimes brutal, examination of witnesses, they began to build a recognizably modern trial procedure. Indeed, the rise of the criminal bar in these trials fostered a new literary genre—a distant ancestor of Erle Stanley Gardner's Perry Mason stories. "The 1780s and 1790s saw the rise of the trial advocate as a virtuoso performer whose words and exploits were to be savored. . . . Their doings were reported in increasing detail, and it was their adversarial achievement as questioners and strategists that began to be the center of attention" in the popular news accounts of trials.[17] Lawyers prepared evidence and questioned witnesses before trial, cross-examined each other's witnesses in front of the jury, and addressed the court on points of law.

Going beyond the unofficial English practice, colonial law stipulated that criminal defendants had a right to be represented by lawyers, a signal advantage to the accused not extended to English felony suspects until 1836. The Massachusetts Body of Liberties, followed by Connecticut's Fundamental Laws, suggested that there was a right to counsel. The Concessions of the West Jersey Proprietors, in 1677, and the Frame of Government of Pennsylvania, in 1683, gave the same assurances. After the dissolution of the first charter, Massachusetts' General Court tried to reenact a guarantee of counsel in 1692, but for other reasons the statute was disallowed by the Privy Council. In 1701, the General Court repassed the criminal counsel provisions, and the courts, on occasion, appointed counsel for needy suspects in felony trials. Connecticut also appointed counsel for indigent defendants in some capital cases. Pennsylvania in 1718, Delaware in 1719, and South Carolina in 1731 wrote explicit provisions for counsel in criminal cases into their laws. Some colonies resisted this reform—New York most notably—but by the 1760s, counsel was permitted felony suspects in more than half the colonies.

The advantage of having a right to counsel was obvious. Counsel could argue the law to the bench and cross-examine witnesses. They could address juries when the defendant was unable to speak persuasively. Andrew Hamilton, one of Philadelphia's foremost lawyers, told a jury: "A proper confidence in a court is commendable; but as the verdict (whatever it is) will be yours, you ought to refer no part of your duty to the discretion of other persons [even the judge!]. If you should be of opinion that there is no falsehood in [the defendant's] papers, you will, nay (pardon me for the expression) you ought to say so; because you don't know whether others (I mean the court) may be of that opinion. It is your right to do so, and there is much depending upon your resolution as well as upon your integrity."[18] What suspect would be likely to speak so well and so convincingly in his or her own case? The defendant, newspaper editor John Peter Zenger, was acquitted.

Andrew Hamilton was not the only colonial lawyer whose reputation before a jury commended him to the attention of defendants. Many, less celebrated, still profited from the colonial right to counsel. When North Carolina lawyer Waitstill Avery successfully defended Paul Crosby against a charge of petty larceny, besting Samuel Spencer, a future supreme court judge, he was "surrounded with a flood of clients and employed this term in no less than 30 actions."[19] After surveying the experience of criminal defendants in Massachusetts' courts over the first half of the eighteenth century, David Flaherty concluded that "suspects were wise to depend on the practical experience and technical knowledge of a trial lawyer. . . . The contrast with the plight of those tried for witchcraft in 1692 and 1693 is evident."[20]

JURIES

The colonists' earliest laws guaranteed jury trials in criminal cases as well as civil suits, and colonial juries may have taken advantage of lay judges to carve out a larger role for juries in criminal trials than they had in England. The first criminal statutes in New England, the work of the Pilgrims, declared that all facts in cases of crime were to be determined by juries. In Massachusetts, a strong magisterial tradition worked against jury trial—Governor John Winthrop regarded judges as "Gods upon earthe" dispensing both mercy and justice—but his fellow freemen demanded and won jury trial of civil and criminal cases.

The criminal jury was a redoubt that the colonists hotly defended against their own magistrates and English authorities, but the reason for this loyalty is not altogether clear. In fact, few accused took advantage of their right to jury trial for petty offenses—most were heard summarily by the bench. Even in more serious crimes, Virginia defendants did not always insist on a jury trial. Fewer than half of all prosecutions that might have been heard by juries were in fact brought before the jury. Defendants were busy plea-bargaining or trying to avoid the expense of a jury trial (they had to pay for it). In New England, defendants commonly but by no means universally asked for jury trial. In New York, upper-class defendants sought jury trials; lower-class defendants only sometimes did the same. When defendants in capital cases asked for and got a jury trial, juries in Massachusetts, New York, and Virginia convicted defendants as often as they acquitted defendants.

The colonists also appreciated the jury because it empowered the average American freeholder to make law. William Nelson has argued that American juries sometimes found law as well as facts: "Juries rather than judges spoke the last word on law enforcement in nearly all, if not all, of the American colonies."[21] In one famous case, publisher John Peter Zenger's trial for a seditious libel of Governor William Cosby of New York, the jury, despite clear instructions from Justice James Delancey (to be sure a crony of Governor Cosby), decided that truth was a defense against seditious libel. In 1771, John Adams applied the same principles to a case of ordinary debt:

> The general Rules of Law and common Regulations of Society, under which ordinary Transactions arrange themselves, are well enough known to ordinary Jurors. The great Principles of the Constitution, are intimately known, they are sensibly felt by every Briton. . . . Now should the Melancholly Case arise, that the Judges should give their Opinions [on the law] to the Jury, against one of these fundamental Principles, is a Juror obliged to give his Verdict generally according to this Direction. . . . [?] Every Man of any feeling or Conscience will answer, no. It is not only his right but his Duty in that Case to find the Verdict according to his own best understanding, Judgment and Conscience, tho in Direct opposition to the Direction of the Court.[22]

In mid-century the jury system faltered in New York, Virginia, and North Carolina. Sheriffs were increasingly hard-pressed to find freeholders willing to serve on juries. In 1741, the New York assembly ordered fines for "remiss" jurors. The act evidently made little impression on the recalcitrant jurors and had to be renewed throughout the 1750s and 1760s. This trend reversed itself on the eve of the Revolution, as juries became part of the apparatus the patriots used to organize resistance to British authorities.

Verdicts of juries and (in "bench trials") findings of judges varied according to the nature of the offense and the jurisdiction in which it occurred. The more serious the offense, the more likely the accused was to be found not guilty. Rates of conviction varied from the middle 30 percent range in Rhode Island, through 40–50 percent in New York and Virginia, to a high of 51 percent in Massachusetts. One must bear in mind, weighing these figures, that many suspects had already slipped from the net because grand juries found "no bill" or because judges dismissed the case for technical reasons. Even so, the conviction rates are two to three times higher than modern felony trial conviction rates.

CRIMINAL PENALTIES

For those convicted at trial, punishment was swift and highly visible. N. E. H. Hull depicted the setting in her work on serious crime in colonial Massachusetts: "Punishment is the most visible proof of the efficacy of the justice system. . . . Only a few men and women could crowd into the courts to hear a sentence spoken, but many could and did attend the punishments. . . . At this stage of the criminal process the court no longer focused solely upon the individual defendant but upon the offense—and all offenses like it. Punishment became an expression of community censure, and the defendant a symbol of disorder, violence, and sin." To the pillory or the gallows went the convict, watched by a throng of officials, ministers, and bystanders. "The message of the pain and shame of punishment" could be and was meant to be seen by all.[23]

At the end of the criminal procedure as at its onset, status mattered. In Massachusetts, servants, Indians, and slaves received many more lashes than others convicted of the same crime. In North Carolina, the master class was fined and the servant class whipped for similar offenses. Sometimes this variation in punishment was built into the law; sometimes it was left to the discretion of judges and magistrates. These officers were always men, and though there is little evidence that they conspired to mistreat women, the poorest women, servant girls and older widows, fared even worse than men under the penal laws. Proved to have concealed the deaths of their bastard infants, some were punished for murder. No man faced that risk. Proved to have "the devil's mark" on their bodies, they faced punishment for witchcraft. No man was examined for such marks. Overwhelmingly, they bore the pain and shame of punishment for bearing the bastard children of their "betters." Convicted by all-male juries and sentenced by male judges for crimes that men defined and prosecuted, women were defamed as symbols of the inherent immorality of a weaker sex.

SLAVERY

The most striking American exception from English law was chattel slavery. Slavery was common in African, Asian, and Mediterranean societies but had no foothold in English law. The labor shortage in some of the colonies was chronic, however, and colonial economies depended upon agricultural productivity. The natural increase of farm families provided cheap labor in New England. The middle colonies were warehouses of immigrant population, filled with young men and women from Scotland, Ireland, and Germany. Although southern tobacco and rice planters pleaded for indentured servants and eagerly put to work those who came, life in Maryland, the coastal areas of Virginia, and, later in the century, the Carolina settlements was never hospitable to the indentured servants. Only a few of those who survived the hardships of their servitude and the "agues and fevers" of the Chesapeake became competitors of the large planters; most moved west and south seeking a new start.

A crisis in agricultural production on the large southern plantations thus loomed by the 1680s. Tobacco prices were falling, and the cost of labor for tobacco, a labor-intensive crop, had become a critical element in the continued profitability of southern staple-crop agriculture. The planters tried to enslave the Indians, but the experiment failed. They would later import more and more "transported" convict laborers and live in fear of crime, though in fact "very few convicts of all those transported to the Chesapeake were ever prosecuted for committing felonies or misdemeanors . . . the large majority of criminal acts were committed by other, 'more respectable' segments of the colonial population, even in areas where convict concentrations were heaviest."[24]

Overwhelmingly, planters turned to the West Indian solution: massive importation of Africans. "Slavery made possible the restoration and maintenance of a highly productive population."[25] Afro-Americans could be pitted against newly arrived Africans and Guineans against captives taken from the Ivory Coast. Originally regarded as indentured servants, Africans were progressively debased by their masters' law. Africans became servants for life, then slaves. The Dutch and later the English made fortunes transshipping captives from West Africa and the West Indies to Virginia and the Carolinas. The trade appealed particularly to capital-starved New England merchants. Soon slave ships from Boston and Newport, Rhode Island, were plying the "middle passage" between the west coast of Africa and the colonies.

Borrowing from the laws of Barbados and Jamaica, English West Indian sugar islands on which African slaves averaged life spans of less than two years, the burgesses of Virginia gradually but inexorably elaborated a system of chattel slavery that had no precedent in English law. These "black codes" made color the badge of slavery. Slaves were property to be bought and sold, given away and inherited. In 1662, the

Virginia House of Burgesses made the condition of mulatto children dependent on the status of the mother, diverging from the patrilineal descent decreed by English law. Slave masters henceforth could claim as slaves the offspring of their illicit unions with female slaves. In 1667, the burgesses reminded masters that baptism of slaves did not elevate them from slavery. In 1669, the assembly prospectively exculpated masters who killed a slave in the course of "due correction." In 1680, the legislature made it a felony for slaves to carry a weapon, leave the plantation without a pass, offer resistance against any free person, or lurk about, the last an open-ended offense capable of infinite extension, punishment for all of which was thirty lashes on the back "well laid on." Later criminal statutes elaborated this law, effectually denying Africans and Afro-Americans the basic rights of any white inhabitant of the English colonies: jury trial by peers when accused of a serious crime, compulsory process against accusers, the right to counsel, and the right to address the court in their own behalf under oath.

The "black codes" these assemblies composed blurred the line between public and private lawmaking. The legislators were slaveholders, and in writing the codes they were protecting their own property. They had a direct, private interest in restraining the will of African-Americans and limiting the rights that they could claim. If one regards the Virginia House of Burgesses as a gathering of property holders meeting together to make mutually beneficial arrangements for one another's private property, one can categorize the black codes as private lawmaking. At the same time, these assemblies were the legislative branch of the colonial government, and bills passed in them, the governor assenting, were law. By enacting the black codes the planter-burgesses made private interest into public policy.

Whites who maimed or killed slaves could not always avert punishment by claiming that they were insulted or that the slave had misbehaved—the burgesses drew the line at their overseers' brutality. When, in August 1743, the justices of the peace in Richmond County brought overseer William Lee into court to answer for killing Will, a slave, with two hundred lashes with a cat-o'-nine-tails and a cowskin whip, Lee answered that he was merely correcting a rebellious bondsman. Lee averred that Will was "very stubborn," and correction was necessary. The justices of the peace thought otherwise; Lee was bound over to stand trial at Williamsburg for manslaughter. Lee had exceeded the bounds and was called to account, but had Will beaten William Lee to death, the trial would have been swift and the punishment, hanging and dismemberment, sure.[26] Two months later, in North Carolina, Matthew Hardy beat his slave Lucy and then tied her to a ladder and burned her to death; he was discharged without punishment. In North Carolina, killing a slave did not become a felony until 1774.[27]

The law of slavery spoke to the master as well as to the slave. The master was given discretion to control the body as well as the time, space, and labor of the slave. Those free persons who challenged the black codes were ostracized or criminally punished. Too often to suit the planters, white servants found common interests with slaves. Humane masters also softened the rigors of slavery, even freeing their slaves, though colonial policy frowned on manumission and slave codes for a time forbade it. As Winthrop Jordan has written, the master was "*required* to punish his runaways, prevent assemblages of slaves, enforce the curfews, sit on the special courts and ride the patrols,"[28] at best a burden in time and expense for very busy men, at worst an invitation to brutality and guilt.

Although whites made and read the laws, the laws themselves were fashioned in part in response to the slaves' behavior. They resisted slavery and brought down upon themselves and the generations of slaves who followed the wrath of the courts. In trying to be free, they forged stronger shackles upon their limbs. Such ironies went everywhere in an economic system whose profits rested on slavery.

All over the South chattel slavery spread, and with it a concept of bondage wholly without precedent in English law and exceeding in severity Roman, Dutch, French, and Spanish law, as well as the laws of Islam and the customs of many African tribes. Nevertheless, chattel slavery well fit an emerging transatlantic commodities market. The great southern planters would become one of the wealthiest groups of agriculturalists in the world.

Few slaves came to the hinterlands of western New York, Pennsylvania, and New Jersey, but slaves were brought to the port cities of the North: New York City, Philadelphia, Newport, and Boston. By the middle of the eighteenth century, slaves constituted nearly 20 percent of the male work force of New York City and Philadelphia. New Englanders bought few slaves, in large measure because New Englanders did not have the capital to sink into the purchase of slaves, in part because the land and the growing season did not return investments in chattel bondsmen and women. Wherever slavery went, there followed some variant of the black codes.

The Slave Conspiracy of 1741, in New York City, graphically demonstrated the corrupting effect of slavery on law. In the 1720s and 1730s, New York City had been the site of a series of minor crime waves involving slaves, free blacks, and whites. In April 1741, eight fires within five days seriously frightened New York City's inhabitants. Suspicious city officials were informed that the fires were part of a slave uprising set in motion at an alehouse by the docks. The white alehouse keeper, John Hughson, was a suspected burglar himself, and at his tavern gathered free blacks and slaves. Rumors became accusations, then grand jury indictments. Trials quickly followed, at the end of which thirteen blacks were burned at the stake for treason, sixteen slaves were hanged along with four whites for arson, and more than seventy blacks were banished from the colony. Along with the slaves, Roman Catholics were persecuted. They too were "others," defined by negation as dangerous deviants on the edge of proper society and always suspected of evil designs against His Majesty's Protestant colonies. Justice Daniel Horsmanden, who sentenced many of the convicts, regarded the slaves as poor wretches but aimed much of his fire at the colonial assembly for not passing a stringent black code.[29] He insisted that blacks—free or slave—who lived among whites always had to be watched.

In his account of the slave trials, Horsmanden insisted that every opportunity was given the defendants to exonerate themselves and all were accorded the full protection of the English law. At best, his protestations were naive. The slaves were not only accused of arson, but of petty treason—doing harm to their masters. Slaves convicted of petty treason were dismembered. New Yorkers' fear of arson was well grounded, but the dismemberment of slaves for treason gives a clue that something more was at stake. There was no ban in the city against slaves congregating in groups of three or more, or requirement that slaves abroad at night have passes from their masters. Such a system could not have worked in a densely packed, commercial community. Slaves in New York City could not be watched and controlled as they could be on the plantation. The show trial of the slaves in 1741 worked as a substitute for more stringent slave law. The trials were designed to reassert the masters' control over the slaves as well as to provide a means to determine innocence and guilt.

To slave defendants unused to the formalities of law and confronted with an outraged community of white property holders who wanted to punish the guilty more than they wanted to ensure the safety of the innocent, Horsmanden's idea of due process could have had little weight. True, in quieter times there were lawyers and judges who tried to protect slaves and promote freedom. George Wythe and Thomas Jefferson in Virginia, for example, argued a series of cases *in forma pauperis* (without payment) for mulattoes trying to free themselves from masters. In *Howell v. Netherland* (1770), Jefferson even lectured the General Court on the barbarity of assuming that the offspring of a woman set free at the age of thirty-five should have to remain a slave until he or she too was thirty-five.[30] He lost the case, however. The court construed the applicable statute to require every mulatto to remain in bondage until that age. The court's construction of the statute's application was probably consistent with its framers' intent; a legislature of slaveholders would not have asked masters to forgo the additional years of mulattoes' servitude.

On the eve of the Revolution, a strong tide of abolitionist sentiment was sweeping the northern cities, in part inspired by the continuing efforts of the Quakers, in part motivated by the reverse of the labor shortage that had, a hundred years before, induced Virginia planters to adopt chattel slavery. In the aftermath of the French and Indian War, there was not enough work for free laborers in New York City, Philadelphia, Boston, and their satellite towns. Slaves competed with free artisans, shipbuilders, construction workers, cartmen, and other "mechanicks" for day labor. The continuing depression meant that merchants and farmers could not compete with southern planters to pay the price for slaves. In the North slavery began to die an economic death similar to that later forecast, incorrectly, for slavery in the South with the crash of tobacco prices after the revolutionary war.

The Paradoxes of the Law

Colonial law at mid-century was riven with paradoxes. With Anglicization in the law came needed sophistication and unwanted formality. Lawyers were everywhere abused for stirring up suits, and everywhere employed to bring suits. The openness and fluidity of the law gave rise to a litigiousness that flooded court dockets and delayed legal redress. The iniquities of private law became the inequities of public law in what seemed to contemporaries to be a spiral of private avarice and official corruption. The law promoted greater equality for some and progressively debased others into chattel slaves.

These tensions in the American law could not be wholly contained within the colonial legal system. Slave rebellions and laboring people's protests erupted periodically, challenging the very foundations of law and order. Popular dissent took other forms as well. In a series of local protests, tenant farmers and small landowners demanded that law conform to local needs. When the landlords of the great manors on east side of the Hudson River refused to allow extensions on past-due rents for their tenants, the tenants rose up in rebellion. Colonial property law favored the landlords; the tenants rested their claims on custom and tradition. The "regulators" of the western Carolinas wanted greater voice in the governance of the colony and protection against the bands of robbers who wandered the Piedmont hill country. In Virginia, grand jurors refused to serve. In a voluntaristic, face-to-face society, growing indifference to public duties was calamitous. Parliament would shortly add to these local disorders the burden of almost unenforceable customs regulations and taxes. A crisis of law and order fast approached the colonies.

"On What Principles, Then, on What Motives of Action, Can We Depend for the Security of our Liberties, of our Properties . . . of Life Itself?"

The litigation explosion and the rise of the lawyers had two dramatic consequences. First, Americans became increasingly conscious of the power and importance of law. They went to court often and came away familiar with the way in which lawyers used arguments. Familiarity bred content, if not always with lawyers, then with law. Americans began to believe that complex social problems had, or ought to have, legal solutions. Second, the litigation explosion had made lawyering a lucrative and respectable profession. The sons of wealthy and well-connected parents had opted for full-time careers in law. Many of these young men would rise to the top of the profession and, joining professional achievement and local eminence, enter politics.

The two direct repercussions of the litigation explosion combined into a third, even more striking consequence. Americans began to see imperial politics in legalistic terms and to approach political disputes with the crown as though they were legal contests. At the same time, certain kinds of legal cases, particularly those involving collection of fees and fines due the crown and its agents, became politicized. Politicization of legal quarrels in the colonies gave lawyers still more influence in public decision making. The continual blurring of the public and the private spheres of law encouraged lawyers to reach into and apply English political theory and jurisprudence to cases and controversies in American courts. Practicing lawyers faced with essentially political quarrels essayed constitutional arguments, tactics that carried the law beyond the courtroom into the streets. Battles over the powers of the branches of government originating in legislatures led to courtroom tests in a continuing round of highly charged interchanges between law and politics.

The revolutionary crisis of 1763–76 was the dramatic, ironic final act in the amalgamation of political methods and legal reasoning, a merger of politics and law at the highest levels of theory and practice. At the very moment that the American legal profession was establishing itself as the gatekeeper—the interpreter and preserver—of a safe and settled Anglo-American legal culture, English authorities were discussing the imposition of new Navigation Acts on the colonies. In the wake of the French and Indian War, the English public debt had soared, and George Grenville's ministry introduced in Parliament laws designed to multiply American contributions to the imperial treasury. While not quite amounting to the plot to destroy colonial liberties which some incendiaries immediately decried, the Sugar Act of 1764 and the Stamp Act of 1765 brought with them a new way of looking at law—an administrative approach—which would have greatly modified the common-law forms to which the colonists and their lawyers were accustomed. New customs regulations imposed a more impersonal and expensive bureaucracy upon colonial shippers and importers. The Stamp Act created another tier of imperial officialdom and burdened every colonist with an internal levy. Colonial mobs took to the streets in Boston, New York City, and Charleston to prevent stamp collectors from doing their job, and village greens served as marshaling grounds of protest against the obnoxious statute. Local law enforcement officials could not check the disorder, nor could courts, without stamps, perform their functions. A political controversy had become a fundamental challenge to law and order.

Colonial legal leaders joined in the controversy. At first, regarding themselves as spokesmen for Anglo-American legal culture, they assumed that they could alter policy in the metropolitan center. They failed and were drawn into the maelstrom of protest. Resistance became revolution. Reluctantly at first, later with éclat, a portion of the American bar crafted elegant briefs exonerating the protesters. This paradox—rebellion justified in the name of law—tested the strength of Americans' commitment to law and encouraged Americans' quest for new and more representative methods of lawmaking.

The Legality of Revolution

As the revolutionaries cast off imperial authority and dispossessed thousands of men and women who remained loyal to the king, Loyalists were quick to cry out that many revolutionary lawyers had taken solemn oaths or affirmations to the crown. Some had held imperial office or colonial office under imperial supervision. All had studied and practiced the common law. How could they participate in the violent closing of royal courts and the overthrow of royal governments? The Loyalists' answer—that the serpent of pride and ambition had crept into Eden—masked both the genuine dilemma of the revolutionary lawyers and the great achievement of revolutionary lawmaking.

To be sure, the Loyalists had on their side the authority of the most respected of all contemporary commentators on English law, William Blackstone of Oxford University. Blackstone, whose massive *Commentaries* on English law (1765–69) was cited on both sides of the Atlantic, viewed law as both the giver and the limiter of liberty. For him, the two functions were inseparable. "This liberty, rightly understood," Blackstone lectured at Oxford in 1758, "consists in the power of doing whatever the law permits; which is only to be effected by a general conformity of all orders and degrees to those equitable rules of action, by which the meanest individual is protected from the insults and oppression of the greatest. . . . therefore every subject [citizen of England] is interested in the preservation of the laws."[1] Political upheaval, even in the name of the greater good of the commonweal, crippled law.

The American protesters could retort that law and revolution were often fellow travelers in English history. Successful rebellions against kings and their governments were never the work of anarchists, and lawyers played a vital role as advocates of the new political order even as the old was crumbling. As Blackstone knew, lawyers had participated in the English revolutions of 1640–60 and 1688–90. Parliament had no sooner made it impossible for King Charles i to govern than lawyers in it set about rewriting the law to make Parliament itself the great "representative" of the people. In the "Glorious Revolution" of 1689, lawyers in Parliament again fully merged politics and lawmaking.

The gradual, often unpredictable elucidation of fundamental law doctrine in England during its civil wars in the seventeenth century fostered a vast literature on constitutional law. Legal thinking over that course of years was a treasury of doctrine and analogy available long after the Civil War and the Stuarts were gone from the scene. There unfolded a "community of discourse" among succeeding generations of lawyers and jurists using many of the same words, often in different ways, always in slightly altered contexts. Crucial misunderstandings were as much a part of this transmission and deployment of legal ideas as were consistent themes and persistent questions, but over the course of two centuries a core theory of good government emerged.

The linchpin of this theory was that government must be accountable to the people. The exercise of power must represent the will of the people. From English jurists, notably Chief Justice Edward Coke, Americans learned that a fundamental law more basic than parliamentary statutes and the decrees of the courts and the crown embodied the ideal of accountability. This fundamental law was a standard against which to measure the actions of those in power. Should the government abuse its trust by ignoring the best interests of the people or succumbing to avarice and ambition, the people might resist the government in the name of that fundamental law. "The right of resistance . . . was still viable in the mid-eighteenth century, providing a legal basis for the argument that Parliament could not exceed its constitutional powers and implying that it was somehow accountable if it did."[2]

Colonial lawyers did not confine their reading to a set canon of legal authorities. Instead, they consumed ideas omnivorously and voraciously. They read Greek and Latin treatises on government and law (the revolutionary lawyers were classically educated; they could quote—or mangle—Thucydides and Cicero as well—or as ineptly—as any of their countrymen); histories of England and Europe; the writings of French and Italian statesmen; essays by the English seventeenth-century republicans John Milton, James Harrington, and Algernon Sidney; the treatises of John Locke; and the letters, pamphlets, and miscellanies of the radical "commonwealthmen" of the eighteenth century who set themselves up as guardians of the English constitution against corrupters in and out of government. Finally, the lawyers consumed the moralizing philosophies, histories, and legal tracts of eighteenth-century Scottish enlightenment thinkers.

A Lawyer's Lexicon for Resistance

Almost all of the revolutionary leaders exhibited what Bernard Bailyn has called an "offhand familiarity" with the great defenders of the common law, venerated Coke, and displayed great erudition in the law.[3] The lawyers within the ranks of the revolutionaries, predisposed by training, intellectual and professional habits, and experience in the courts to think in legal terms, were willing and able to do more than give lip service to the task of legalizing the protest. Despite the variety of the sources they used, American revolutionary lawyers read and debated political philosophy, history, and law as lawyers. They thought like lawyers, not political philosophers, or disinterested scholars, or "Pennsylvania Farmers" (to use lawyer John Dickinson's nom de plume), or public-spirited lay persons. They joined the legal and political arguments into a powerful defense of rebellion.

Common-law pleaders, the revolutionary lawyers naturally first turned to common law to promote their cause. From 1763 to 1775, American lawyers ransacked common law to find evidence against parliamentary impositions. The major obstacle they faced was that Parliament was not only a maker of statutes, it was also the highest common-law court in the land. Undeterred, like every good counselor in the service of a client, the American revolutionary lawyers sought to distinguish their case from earlier colonial claims rejected by Parliament and the crown. If common law was what English authorities said it was, a coil in the cord that bound the subordinate colonies to a dominant metropolitan center of power, the lawyers would fashion an American common law that was part of the longer cord but still gave Americans freedom to protest parliamentary impositions.

The obstacles in their path were enormous. Common law was disseminated in reports of judges' opinions. The common-law reports that circulated throughout the colonies were written in England, by English judges or their clerks, and contained English cases. These might or might not be applicable to private-law disputes in the colonies, but in and of themselves they provided no precedent for political dissent. American judges did not publish reports of their opinions because few American appellate court judges wrote opinions. Standing at the bar, colonial lawyers could rely on English reports to cite English cases, but the colonial lawyers learned about American judicial precedents through word of mouth.

The absence of controlling opinions from American colonial high courts may be explained in another way. Under imperial law, the American colonies were not sovereignties, and therefore all American courts might be regarded as trial courts (much as county superior courts today), not appellate courts. The willingness of American supreme courts to allow suits to be reheard in their entirety was evidence for this proposition. Decisions of cases in trial courts do not become rules for other courts as do the opinions of appellate courts. Thus, even had the colonial supreme court judges written and published their opinions, these opinions would not have had the weight of opinions issued by the courts at Westminster.

The lawyers could argue that individual colonies had carved out for themselves small areas of exception from English common law, largely through custom and statute rather than judicial opinion. The rules of partible inheritance in New England, for example, fit this description. These rules were limited, however, to the jurisdiction from which they came and applied to narrow questions. Such intracolonial variances from English common law did not amount to an American common law, much less give foundation to claims that American law and customs might supersede directives from England.

American lawyers' briefs offered an unofficial but widely circulated and closely read source of law which the dissidents might employ in the absence of judicial opinions. In cases of great constitutional moment colonial lawyers often published their speeches to the judges and the jury. These were consulted throughout the colonies and might be regarded as applicable to broad public questions. The first of these publications antedated the final crisis but were well known to every revolutionary lawyer. James Alexander's account of the Zenger trial, featuring Andrew Hamilton's arguments on the crime of seditious libel, was one such brief. So was Judge Lewis Morris's account of his opposition to Governor Cosby's plan for an exchequer court in New York.

There followed, at first sporadically and then with greater regularity as the crisis grew, lawyers' accounts of arguments against the writs of assistance, stamp taxes, and the Townshend duties. The authors of these briefs were working lawyers such as Daniel Dulany, Jr., of Maryland, James Otis, Jr., of Massachusetts, John Dickinson and James Wilson of Pennsylvania, Thomas Jefferson, and John Adams. Sometimes these publications originated in a real case or controversy in court; sometimes they anticipated such a case. The pamphlets that were to become the staple of revolutionary propaganda featured an extended exchange of legal ideas and functioned as a surrogate for an American common law. Some of these pamphlets, written in haste early in the crisis by leading lawyers such as James Otis, Jr., and Daniel Dulany, Jr., actually looked and sounded like briefs. Later pamphleteers camouflaged their legal training (John Dickinson styled his objections to parliamentary legislation *Letters from a Pennsylvania Farmer*), but their work retained its legal character.

Briefing the Case for Colonial Rights

Four court cases—the "Parson's Cause" in Virginia, the Writs of Assistance case in Massachusetts, McDougall's case in New York, and, in somewhat more complex fashion, the Boston Massacre trials—demonstrated how the arguments of lawyers at trial could feed into and be magnified by quarrels over politics and become part of an American common law. Not surprising, all four cases inched the lawyers involved toward further protest activities. By channeling protest into the courts, lawyers could control the flow of public protest and prevent the mob from turning against all their "betters." Lawyers, drawn from the elite of society, preferred known law to the uncertain outcome of street politics.

The Parson's Cause was a Virginia case. Like England, Virginia had an established church. The salaries of the Virginia ministers of the Church of England were calculated in terms of tobacco. As tobacco prices on the international market varied, so did the returns to the Virginia tobacco planters for their crops, but the legislature artificially pegged the value of tobacco for the purpose of paying the ministers. In 1758, beset by the ravages of the French and Indian War, unsure of the future of tobacco, challenged by Baptist dissenters in the backwoods parishes, patronized and criticized by the great planters in their congregations, the Virginia ministers learned that they would only be getting 2 pence to the pound of tobacco as their salary. They complained to the House of Burgesses, got nowhere, and wrote remonstrances to the king's Privy Council. Three years later the Privy Council declared the "Two Penny Act" null and void. Legally, the act had never been in effect.

A number of ministers sued their parishes for back pay. Juries in these trials could hardly deny the ministers damages, but in one case, *Maury v. Parish of Fredericksville* (1762), the minister plaintiff ran into a young lawyer with political ambitions and unique rhetorical skills. Patrick Henry represented the parish and astutely turned a private suit for back pay into a contest over the rights of Englishmen—in particular, the rights of the parish's planters to dispose of their property as they chose. Henry argued that the voters' will, expressed in the Two Penny Act, should not have been disallowed by the Privy Council. Despite cries of "treason, treason" from opposing counsel, Henry continued that the people ought to have the right to make their own laws. The jury returned with damages of one penny for Reverend Maury, a victory that propelled Henry into the front rank of the bar and demonstrated that there was no clear line—not for a zealous advocate— between private disputes and public questions in Virginia.

Meanwhile, in Massachusetts, customs collector Charles Paxton and his associates were making a living for themselves from the fees they received for catching smugglers. Earlier customs officials had accepted bribes to look the other way, but Paxton wanted to do his job. Massachusetts merchants regularly smuggled molasses, tea, and other commodities purchased from the French, Dutch, and Spanish into local ports. The only way to make charges against smugglers stick was to obtain evidence of goods brought into the colony illegally. The customs collectors based their right to search and seize such evidence on both English and colonial statutes and practice. Under the Act to Prevent Fraud of 1660, customs officials could obtain search warrants that specified the items sought and the place to be searched. These searches were to be conducted in daytime (to avert the possibility of an official being mistaken for a burglar). If the informant's "tip" proved false, however, the injured party could sue the informant for damages. In 1662 a second act of Parliament gave further authority for forcible entry of suspected customs dodgers' premises. In 1696, the Admiralty Act extended these statutes to the colonies, along with eleven "vice-admiralty courts" ready and willing to hear cases without juries and punish offenders. Mid-eighteenth-century English excise laws added a new dimension to search and seizure. To find evidence of evasion of the taxes on salt, soap, paper, and apple cider, tax collectors were permitted to break into private dwellings without fear of legal reprisal.

Almost all of the colonies allowed customs officials and magistrates to search and seize evidence in criminal cases under a search warrant. The Massachusetts "writ of assistance" was drafted by a lawyer, Edmund Trowbridge, from a model he found in a book of English writs. Unfortunately, he chose a writ for inspection of customs at the English port of Dover which was already out of date in England, and worse, Trowbridge did not fully adapt the Dover writ to the Massachusetts situation. It was this writ that was in use in the 1750s, however, without much protest from anyone.

In December 1760, Paxton and the other collectors of customs had to obtain new writs of assistance—the old ones, issued under the authority of George II, now dead, died with him. Stephen Sewall, the chief justice of the Superior Court of Judicature and a much-loved old man, but never a trained lawyer, had refused to issue the new writs until the full court could assemble for a hearing on the question of whether the court had jurisdiction to issue such writs. The underlying, vexatious question was which courts should hear disputed customs cases—common-law courts like the Superior Court of Judicature which impaneled juries or vice-admiralty courts that did not.

Before the court could meet, Sewall died, and Governor Francis Bernard named a new chief justice, merchant Thomas Hutchinson. Hutchinson came from one of the wealthiest and best politically connected families in the colony but was hotly opposed by James Otis of Barnstable. Otis had been promised the post by Bernard's predecessors, Governors William Shirley and Thomas Pownall. Bernard did not feel bound by others' patronage arrangements and deemed Hutchinson, though not a lawyer, a safer choice to protect the interests of the crown. The factional forces released by Bernard's decision exploded in the courtroom when Hutchinson convened the Superior Court of Judicature in February 1761 to hear the customs officers argue for their petition.

The customs officials asked Jeremiah Gridley to argue for the writs. He did, citing ample precedent and statutory authority that customs officials had the right to obtain the writ to search suspected violators' premises. Oxenbridge Thacher replied for the merchants, insisting that the writs were overbroad. He had before him evidence that the Massachusetts writs were too general by English standards, perhaps a result of Trowbridge's inept effort to copy the Dover writs. The dispute had political implications—smuggling was to become a patriotic cause— and Gridley and Thacher did not have the last word in the case.

James Otis, Jr., stirred by resentment at the slight to his father as well as by love of colonial rights, had volunteered to join Thacher. When Otis's turn came to address the court, he drove directly to the political question. He spoke for hours, and young John Adams, seated in the back of the courtroom, recalled that no oration ever stirred him more profoundly. Otis insisted that the writs violated fundamental law, the law that controlled the actions of Parliament when that body passed statutes. The fundamental law of England made a man's house his castle, safe from illegal searches and seizures. He conceded that Parliament was supreme yet proclaimed that even Parliament could not transgress the fundamental rights of Englishmen. It was an inconsistent thesis but a galvanizing performance, at least according to John Adams, who recorded the events in his diary.

Hutchinson backed away from the confrontation; he ruled that the customs collectors would have to wait until English procedure was more fully reported in Massachusetts. Six judges, bewigged and richly robed in red, representing the majesty of the common law, believing that the law in England sanctioned the writs, hesitated before an argument resting not on settled points of law but on a constitutional theory of dubious provenance and insidious implication. The Massachusetts Superior Court of Judicature later ruled that the writs were legal, but the writs were never effective again in the Bay Colony.

By the middle 1760s, lawyers representing the protest were becoming adept at using civil and criminal suits to organize and energize opposition to the crown. In McDougall's case, for example, the government of the New York colony was brought to a halt in just such fashion. In December 1769, the assembly voted to provision the English soldiers quartered in the city of New York. The bill outraged the leaders of the Sons of Liberty and its secret patrons, the powerful Livingston family. Alexander McDougall, a ship's captain, self-taught and widely read, wrote and secretly published a pamphlet attacking the bill and its authors, the DeLancey faction in the assembly. The majority of the assembly voted the pamphlet a libel of its privileges and set about bribing every printer's devil in the city to find out who printed the piece. One of them informed on James Parker, who had printed McDougall's assault, and Parker, threatened with fines and jail, gave the assembly McDougall's name. Indicted for the crime of seditious libel by a grand jury friendly to the DeLanceys (indeed, handpicked by their ally, the sheriff), McDougall demanded a jury trial in the supreme court and refused to post bail. The sheriff carted McDougall off to jail.

McDougall was already a hero to the Sons of Liberty and made himself a martyr to the cause by refusing bail. For eighty days he sat in jail, while his supporters used his cause to embarrass the DeLanceys and their pro-English party in the city of New York. McDougall was not tried in court (Parker died before he could testify), but shortly after he was freed on the seditious libel charge, the assembly itself imprisoned him for contempt. While McDougall languished for twelve more weeks in the jail, his legal counsel, John Morin Scott, William Smith, Jr., and William Livingston—the "triumvirate" of Whig lawyers in New York—turned the political controversy over the Quartering Act into a test of legal rights. McDougall's case had become a symbol of the way in which a supposedly corrupt majority in the assembly could conspire with judges and a governor chosen by the crown to violate the rights of the people. The courtroom was to be his rostrum. In the end, the pro-British faction in the assembly was fortunate that McDougall never got his day in court. With Scott, Smith, and Livingston ready to take the government to court, Governor William Tryon and his allies in the assembly might well fear the outcome of a legal contest with the "triumvirate."

The Boston Massacre of 1770, as patriot propagandists called it, began with a snowball fight and ended with the death of five Bostonians.

At the request of Governor Bernard, regular British troops were sent to Boston in 1769. Quarrels over housing the troops, disputes over the soldiers' off-hours occupations and conduct, and ridicule of the officers by the "mechanicks," apprentices, and day laborers led to street fights, name calling, and misdemeanor charges against some of the troops. Angry at their treatment in the civil courts of the town, gangs of soldiers began their own little war. The town's young men retaliated in kind. Truces arranged by both sides were undermined by the agitation of the radicals, in particular Samuel Adams, and by the attitude of the officers, particularly Colonel William Dalrymple.

On a cold and cloudy night in March, rumors of atrocities by off-duty soldiers led a mob to congregate before a sentry box. The sentry, fearing for his life, called out for assistance, and Captain Thomas Preston led six other soldiers to rescue the sentry. Confronted by an angry mob literally no more than a bayonet away, Preston tried to reason his way out of trouble. One of his relief party, a grenadier (a special unit of very tall shock troops), was knocked down and rose up firing his musket. A ragged volley followed, no one really sure who ordered the firing. Perhaps the cries of "fire"—used by the mob leaders all night to assemble their followers (the town had no fire brigade and was built of wood; anyone seeing a fire was expected to call out "fire," and bucket brigades then formed)—were misunderstood by the soldiers as an order to discharge their muskets. When the smoke cleared, the soldiers found that the mob was fleeing. Three men lay dead, a fourth was dying, and a fifth, a boy who had come to see but not to join the mob, died two days later.

Captain Preston and his command were indicted for murder. At first, no one could be found to defend them. Wishing to avoid reprisals and sure that a conviction was inevitable, radical leaders prevailed upon two of their number, John Adams and Josiah Quincy, Jr., to represent the British soldiers. Adams later recalled that only his love of rule of law motivated him. At the trial he insisted that the protest movement must rest upon law or fail: "Whatever effect they may have on politics; they are rules of common law, the law of the land." Adams and Quincy, counsel for Preston, cleverly insisted that he should be tried first, separate from his men. Their defense for him was that he did not give the order to fire, in effect that the soldiers acted on their own. Although Adams later claimed that the trial proved the integrity of the revolutionary movement, in fact the jury was packed for the defense. On it sat six known Loyalists. Adams and Quincy could have sat on their hands; the prosecutor (Quincy's brother Samuel, a Loyalist— more irony) had to prove that Preston did give the order to fire and that there was no need for it. Witnesses' testimony was conflicting; they could not even agree on what Preston wore, where he stood, or what he said. There was some evidence that Preston remained in front of his troops, surely a dangerous place to be if he intended them to fire their muskets. Preston was acquitted. The trial of the soldiers turned on a new defense tactic. Adams and Quincy conceded that the soldiers had fired willfully and their fire had killed the five men, but they added that the soldiers feared for their lives, had no place to run, and acted wholly in self-defense. The jury agreed.

During the course of his opening address to the jury in the second trial, Quincy demonstrated the way in which the revolutionary bar used legal occasions to promote revolutionary aims. "I say, Gentlemen, and appeal to you for the truth of what I say, that many on this continent viewed their chains as already forged, they saw fetters as prepared, they beheld the soldiers as fastening and riveting for ages, the shackles of their bondage." Having made his point with this incendiary rhetoric, and no doubt on the verge of censure by the court, Quincy returned to the business of defending the soldiers whose masters in Westminster and Whitehall he had excoriated. "With the justice of these apprehensions, you and I have nothing to do in this place. Disquisitions of this sort are for the Senate . . . they are for statesmen and politicians . . . but we, gentlemen, are confined in our excursions, by the rigid rules of law." Quincy continued in this vein, mixing revolutionary political incitement with admonitions to the jury to leave politics out of their verdict. "Upon the *real, actual* existence of these apprehensions, in the community, we may judge—they are *facts* falling properly within our cognizance . . . but you are to determine on the facts coming to your knowledge [at this trial]—you are to think, judge, and act, as jurymen, and not as statesmen."[4]

In an ironic inversion of Anglicization of the private law, English radicals seeking reform of public law took their cues from the American political trials. Defenders of John Wilkes, whose fame among the revolutionaries would lead them to name towns after him, turned his trial for seditious libel of the crown into a political showcase. His lawyers, part of his circle of admirers and supporters, followed the lead of the colonial Whig bar in making trials into forums for political protest. Returning to England from France in 1768 to stand trial, Wilkes lost his case (he went to jail for twenty-two months), but his supporters found other opportunities to bring charges against royal officials after troops opened fire on demonstrators in St. George's Fields outside London. During these hearings they used the qualified immunity (qualified by the danger of a contempt citation from the judge) which lawyers had in the courtroom to make speeches calling for reform of the courts and Parliament. They demanded in court, as Wilkes had in his earlier North Briton pamphlets—the publications that had first brought him notoriety and landed him in jail—that government be accountable to the people.

From Resistance to Revolution

Royal judges, particularly in Massachusetts, were well aware of the manipulation of law by Whig lawyers. Hutchinson tried to fight back. Like the lawyers for the opposition, Hutchinson saw an essentially political quarrel in legal terms. As he told the grand jury of Suffolk County at its March 1767 session:

> There has been a failure of Law amongst us, which has been very detrimental. Doubts and Differences of Opinion have been, which has caused a great Deal of Confusion. 'Tis to be hoped we are returning again to good Order. I wish the Laws to be put in due Execution for the publick Good, and am as much for the Liberties of the people, as any Man, *so far as is consistent with the Welfare of the Community*. In this Country we have always been happy with a good Set of Laws. The Principle Crown-Law of this Province is grounded on our provincial Laws; where these fail, the Common Law of England is the Rule. The Principle of the Crown-Law is, establishing Punishment, not according to the Degree of moral Evil in the Offense, but according as the Crime affects the peace of the Community.[5]

As Hutchinson defended the interests of the crown in the language of a dutiful magistrate seeking to keep order, protesting lawyers fashioned even more thoroughgoing dissents out of legal ideas. John Dickinson, perhaps the most successful lawyer in the city of Philadelphia, wrote the most admired antiparliamentary pamphlets of the late 1760s. His "Letters" from a "Pennsylvania Farmer" published in the winter of 1767–68, during the scrap over the Townshend duties on tea, glass, and other consumer items, condemned taxation masquerading as trade regulation. Although he claimed to be a mere husbandman, a simple farmer who read the books in his betters' libraries, Dickinson tutored his readers in "the laws and constitution of my county," as though there were an American common law, using all the arts of legal reasoning which had made him so successful in court. He had "looked over every statute relating to these colonies," he reported, and there was "undisputed precedent" against taxation in the "intent" of the framers of the first colonial charters.[6] He concluded that Parliament was engaging in dangerous and unnecessary innovation.

Dickinson's student, James Wilson, a more original thinker than Dickinson though equally cautious in his conduct, thought long and hard about the political crisis before committing anything to paper. In 1768, newly elected to the colonial assembly, he wrote but did not deliver his thoughts on parliamentary exactions: "On what principles, then, on what motives of action, can we depend for the security of our liberties, of our properties . . . of life itself?" "Interest"—a word fraught with meaning for protesters, for it was used very differently by supporters of the English government—did not bind members of Parliament to the needs of the colonies; quite the reverse was true. Members of Parliament were supposed to "represent" the nonvoters of England because members of Parliament had to pay the same taxes and obey the same laws as anyone else, but the colonial Whigs rejected this argument. Powerful English commercial interests, in particular West Indian absentee landlords and their factors (middlemen), saw colonial commercial interests as rivals and bought up parliamentary votes. So did greedy English land speculators who blocked American farmers' migration west. Wilson concluded that "it is repugnant to the essential maxims of jurisprudence, to the ultimate end of all governments, to the genius of the British constitution, and to the liberty and happiness of the colonies, that they should be bound by the legislative authority of Great Britain."[7]

Wilson was uneasy whenever he went near political theory but happily sought and found legal precedent to bolster his argument: in the time of Richard III, the judges of England had declared that parliamentary statute did not run in the king's possessions in Ireland. So, too, the colonists of America were not bound by Parliament. "Permitted and commissioned by the crown, they undertook, at their own expense, expeditions to this distant country, took possession of it, planted it, and cultivated it. Secure under the protection of the king, they grew and multiplied. . . . They inculcated to their children the warmest sentiments of loyalty to their sovereign. . . . Lessons of loyalty to Parliament, indeed they never gave: they never suspected that such unheard of loyalty would ever be required." The king was the giver of common law; under it the colonists claimed the "enjoyment of liberty." Parliamentary statutes were another matter entirely.[8]

Wilson regarded himself as a common lawyer arguing within the framework of an American common law. He did not think of himself as a theorist or of his arguments as metaphors. But if Wilson was right, the charters and grants that inaugurated the colonies took on a new hue. They became part of a transatlantic fundamental law reaching back in time to Magna Charta and forward to the crisis of 1765–76. Against a Parliament whose majority was increasingly indifferent to American claims of right, the American revolutionary lawyer became the great interpreter of a constitution based on fundamental law. The revolutionary lawyers rejected the English imperial ideal of an administrative, centralized state. There was no question that George III and his minions were bent on remodeling the administration of the empire, claiming all the while that they were merely enforcing long-standing imperial rescripts. In the American common law, these novelties were an invasion of old rights, a dangerous invasion of "arbitrary power" threatening the security of property and personal liberty.

It requires a certain amount of scholarly omniscience to decide whether the lawyers for the Revolution could have crafted a winning brief—an argument that would have convinced king and Parliament to withdraw from the Sugar Act, the Stamp Act, and all their progeny. The revolutionary lawyers' initial efforts, grounded on the American common law, could not overcome the intransigence of king and Parliament because king and Parliament were in fact the ultimate arbiters of all common-law actions. English friends of the colonies begged Lord North's ministry not to insist on its legal right to tax the Americans, but North and his allies did not heed such pleas for moderation. Lawyers on both sides of the issue might be excused for missing the irony that, cast as a legal contest in a common-law system, an adversarial system, someone had to win the dispute over taxation. George III's advisers insisted it be Parliament. By framing their protest, at least initially, as a form of courtroom advocacy, the colonists placed themselves in a cul-de-sac. Although the American common lawyers wrote magnificent briefs, the king dismissed the suit.

In the face of this rebuke, the revolutionary lawyers were in a quandary. Were they to continue their advocacy, they would risk the king's displeasure—or worse, prosecution for treason. It may be argued that the lawyers for the revolutionary cause had ceased by 1775 to be lawyers and had become mere partisans—propagandists or prisoners of ideology. More detached counselors might have advised their clients to settle for the best they could get, and that is just what lawyers like Joseph Galloway and William Smith, Jr., said to the Continental Congress. In fact, Lord North did offer the colonies a measure of self-government in 1775, but the Congress summarily rejected the compromise.

No Middle Ground

Between 1773 and 1775, lawyers and judges in the colonies had to choose the law they wanted to defend. The middle ground was disappearing. The revolutionary lawyers did not abandon the common law entirely but used legal modes of reasoning to transform the common law from a body of precedent to an abstract ideal of what good law should be. They fashioned meta-law. Typical of them, James Wilson cut the tie that bound the common law to royal authority and celebrated its general maxims. In an address to the Pennsylvania provincial government, he omitted references to the king's domain because the king had ignored the petitions of his colonial subjects. Instead of the rules of common law, Wilson argued that the "law is a common standard," a type, not a body of particular precepts to which the colonists were obedient. There had been "a great compact between the king and his people," creating a trust, which the king violated when he "altered the charter" of Massachusetts. He was just as bound by the law—not the imperial law, but the immutable principles of trusteeship—as the colonists. With his breach of the trust, the tie of allegiance of colonists to king was also broken. "All attempts to alter the charter or constitution of [a] colony, unless by the authority of its own legislature, are violations of its rights, and illegal." Massachusetts' charter, once a privilege granted by the king, Wilson transmuted into a "constitution" preceding and enabling government, which limited the power of its royal grantor. A now abstract "liberty," freed from the particular constraints of common law, disassociated from common-law texts, directly confronted royal prerogative. Fundamental law was no longer the natural emanation of common law but stood apart and rested upon a gradually solidifying foundation of popular sovereignty.[9]

Royal governors and judges, torn in two directions by their love for the colonies and their loyalty to the crown, were trapped in the wreckage of the imperial system. Hutchinson, elevated to the position of the royal governor of Massachusetts, had found that his assembly would not permit supreme court judges to accept a royal salary. Such a salary would make the judges the tools of Lord North's ministry, the assembly leaders bellowed. When Chief Justice Peter Oliver, a retiring man whose major claim to the office was that he had married Hutchinson's sister, refused to bow to the will of the assembly, the popular party in it began impeachment proceedings against him. Hutchinson blocked the impeachment trial and insisted that the Superior Court of Judicature continue to sit. The judges were uneasy. Oliver refused to come to court, fearing violence against himself.

One of the judges, Edmund Trowbridge, left a firsthand account of what happened next. He told Hutchinson "[that] I was afraid Judge Olivers going to Worcester [to preside at court] would be attended with bad consequences, that there would be no court held while he was there . . . the Governor [Hutchinson] said 'There will be no need of that, I dont think he will go.'" According to Trowbridge, Oliver got as far as a tavern on the road to Worcester and then bolted for home. Meanwhile at court Trowbridge could not get enough jurors to take the oath until they were assured that Oliver was not coming. Finally, late in the afternoon, enough jurors were sworn for the court to begin.[10] Worse was to come for the judges. By the beginning of 1774, they could not hold court safely. The threat of violence, or at least active noncooperation by the community, dissuaded the court from making its rounds of the counties.

That spring a "tea party" held by invitation of the Sons of Liberty at the Boston docks so outraged Lord North and his supporters in Parliament that, after a short and bilious debate, Parliament closed the Port of Boston, causing genuine (if well-orchestrated) outrage throughout the colonies. Massachusetts' royal government, refashioned by Parliament to make it more amenable to imperial decrees, could not keep order in the colony. By the end of 1774, Boston was filled with refugees and soldiers. Whig lawyers had closed up shop. Legal education had come to a standstill. By the time the British troops abandoned Boston in the spring of 1776, many of the city's leading lawyers were quartered in Cambridge, directing the provincial government of the state, or off in Philadelphia, guiding the course of a new nation.

Even lawyers who had been steady for independence had to decide how best to further the cause. John Adams thought long and hard about the role lawyers ought to play in the coming struggle. By 1774, he was acknowledged the leader of the revolutionary bar in his colony and would represent Massachusetts at the Continental Congress in Philadelphia. He knew firsthand how rebellion confuted the normal processes of law—he had defended the British soldiers who fired on the Boston crowd on March 5, 1770, recommended impeachment of Peter Oliver in 1773, and supported the closing of the royal courts in 1775. Adams' correspondence with Jonathan Mason, Jr., a younger Boston lawyer, graphically depicted the crisis state of legal practice. On July 9, 1776, Mason wrote to Adams: "Since my commencement of the Study [of law], I have laboured under many disadvantages. Tho' driven from Boston, tho' at times totally destitute of a patron, I have constantly endeavored to lay a theoretical foundation, but even the minutest forms of practice it has hitherto been impossible to acquire."

Mason, despairing, asked Adams if the latter would recommend that Mason join the Massachusetts contingent in the Continental Army. Adams sternly replied, "I cannot advise you, to quit the retired scene, of which we [lawyers] have hitherto appeared to be so fond, and engage in the noisy business of War. . . . I see no Necessity for it. Accomplishments of the civil and political Kind are no less necessary, for the happiness of Mankind than martial ones. We cannot be all Soldiers, and there will probably be in a very few Years a greater Scarcity of lawyers, and Statesmen than of Warriors."[11] Adams understood that without lawyers carrying on the everyday business of representing clients there could be neither liberty nor property. If the lawyers' higher duty was to vindicate the Revolution, they also must bear the burden of protecting private rights against invasion by private persons.

While Adams waved his pen like a sword, William Smith, Jr., a leader of the New York bar, could not bring himself to choose sides in the final crisis. Although he arrayed himself with the revolutionaries until the eve of the Declaration of Independence, he tried to remain neutral after July 4, 1776. Smith was given sanctuary on the estate of the family of his former revolutionary colleague William Livingston. When warfare worsened between loyalists and revolutionaries in 1777, Smith was forced to choose: pledge allegiance to the state of New York or make his way through the lines to the British authorities in New York City. He elected the latter and for his loyalty to the crown was elevated to the chief justiceship of British Canada.

While Smith dithered, other New York lawyers gravitated toward the revolutionary movement. John Jay, named to the new state supreme court, would later represent the nation in Spain. James Duane and Egbert Benson, like Jay attached to the Livingston political faction, also emerged as powerful figures in the state government. The New York lawyers in the delegation to the Continental Congress, Jay and Duane, were not eager for independence. With Dickinson and Wilson of Pennsylvania, Jay and Duane researched the common law for an alternative to complete separation. Dickinson, the penman of the first two Congresses, searched particularly diligently in his law books and his memory for a way to preserve the peace. John Adams was more forward in countenancing a final breach, joining Thomas Jefferson in the drafting of a legal document declaring independence.

The Greatest of Laws: Constitutions

In the midst of protest, the revolutionaries embarked upon their most audacious legal program, the effort to write state constitutions. The revolutionaries' decision to draft constitutions and found government upon them departed from British legal tradition. To this conclusion the revolutionary lawyers had been driven by the logic of their own protests: law must precede and limit power. If constitutions were needed, John Adams offered to frame them. In April 1776, Adams penned and circulated his own "Thoughts on Government." More a collector of ideas than an original thinker, Adams jumbled traditional elements of English constitutionalism with more forward-looking concessions to centralized, bureaucratic rule. He juggled utilitarianism ("the form of government, which communicates ease, comfort, security, or in one word happiness to the greatest number of persons, and in the greatest degree, is the best") and the commonwealthmen's celebration of disinterested civic virtue ("the noblest principles and most generous affections in our nature then, have the fairest chance to support the noblest and most generous models of government"). The assembly of the new states should be truly representative, a miniature of the people, but its power was to be checked by an upper house elected by the assembly, an independent judiciary, and a strong executive. "The judges therefore should always be men of learning and experience in the laws, of exemplary morals, great patience, calmness, coolness and attention. . . . To these ends they should hold estates for life in their offices, or in other words their commissions should be during good behavior, and their salaries ascertained and established by law."[12] Adams had no use for judges serving at the pleasure of the king, as they had in the Massachusetts colony, living on fees or fines levied on defendants. His vision of professional judiciary did not come to pass in all of the new states but ultimately was enacted in the federal Constitution.

Adams sent copies of his "Thoughts" to Pennsylvania and Virginia, where revolutionaries had called conventions to draft constitutions. Not quite returning to Locke's state of nature to write their fundamental laws (Connecticut and Rhode Island merely restyled their old charters "constitutions"), the revolutionaries nevertheless discarded monarchy in favor of republicanism. The new constitutions featured checks and balances, bills of rights, and provision for regular rotation or removal of incumbent officials. The revolutionaries borrowed many techniques of governance from English and Continental models, but taken as a whole revolutionary constitutionalism was something quite without precedent. American fundamental law made the people sovereign. They had to ratify the new constitutions before they went into effect (except in South Carolina, where a lowland planter aristocracy ensured its own dominance by drafting and adopting a constitution with minimal popular participation). Theoretically, the interests of the people were paramount in these new governments; henceforth, all officials and representatives would be the trustees of the people, acting in the interest of the governed and removable upon demand.

If the language of these documents exhibited great uniformity, there were marked differences in the structures of state governance. Pennsylvania and Georgia fashioned unicameral legislatures with universal male white suffrage, limited the power of courts and magistrates, and inched toward democracy. Pennsylvania mandated popular election of justices of the peace, as far from the original of that office as one could go. New York and South Carolina required that men possess substantial property to hold office and vote. The other states fell between the Pennsylvania and South Carolina extremes. Despite the pleas of able advocates of women's rights like Abigail Adams, no state save New Jersey gave women the right to vote, and New Jersey soon recanted its liberality.

The new state constitutions spoke of the liberty and equality of citizens. The reality was different. Slaves, women, aliens, non-Protestants, Indians, and the poor—the "others" in revolutionary America—were not accorded equal status to free, Protestant men of property. Virginia's Declaration of Rights, the model for other bills of rights, only applied to those "in a state of society"—slaves were legally regarded as outside this sacred circle of citizenship. Women were still legally "covered" by their fathers or spouses, and Indians remained wards of the Congress, permanent strangers in their own land. What Bernard Bailyn has called a "contagion of liberty" began the slow process of disestablishing the churches, freeing some slaves, and promising some measure of equality for women and the poor, but these promises were not fulfilled then and remain in some measure unfulfilled to this day.

Nevertheless, at this distance it is easy to glorify the revolutionary constitutions, and historians have on occasion succumbed to that temptation. For the lawyers and lawmakers in the revolutionary cause, no such innocence was possible. In every bit of territory tenuously held from British arms, the revolutionaries had to re-create government and ensure public order, not only against potential Loyalists but also against common criminals. The revolutionary provincial governments had to replace long-established local and general courts, protect land titles, recover chattels, and exact from citizens the means to carry on a long, bloody, and exhausting war for independence.

The Legislative Mandate

One of the basic principles reflected in the operation and the theory of the new republican governments was the supremacy of the legislature. Despite Adams' admonitions against weakening the executive and judiciary, provincial assemblies took upon themselves the direction of the struggle against Britain. In one sense, that struggle went back to the early eighteenth century, unfolding itself as assemblies coerced, bullied, and bribed royal governors to concede to the assembly the privileges of initiating legislation, naming minor officials, and apportioning the spoils of empire. The controversies of the 1760s transformed these occasional affrays into grim combat over the role of the assembly in the imperial system as a whole. Assemblies questioned the governor's right to dissolve them at his pleasure and the crown's right to tell the governor who should sit in the colonial upper house. Leaders of the lower houses proclaimed the assemblies miniature parliaments, fully capable of making final legislative pronouncements. At the same time, the colonial assemblies increasingly felt danger to their authority from below, for the leaders of the lower house did not want to relinquish direction of the resistance movement to street demonstrators. Against the crown and the crowd the assemblies insisted on the autonomy of their deliberations and the rightness of their cause.

After hostilities commenced, necessity furthered the ascendancy of the assembly. With the royal courts closed and the new state governors or executive committees overwhelmed with the details of carrying on a war, the representative branch shouldered the burden of replacing the partially discarded common law with republican statutes. Even when older colonial precedent was permitted to retain its force, the assembly faced an intellectual and a political challenge of great magnitude.

Three areas of lawmaking required ingenuity and effort from the provincial governments—safeguarding the state, raising funds, and controlling personal conduct. In slightly altered order of priority they had been the same functions that the first colonial governments had to perform. The first of these entailed provision for public officers and proscription of the Loyalists. Almost all of the new states passed legislation continuing local magistrates in office if they subscribed to loyalty oaths. The use of oaths was general throughout the new states—ironic in the light of the revolutionaries' violation of their own oaths to the crown, but practical because an oath was traditional, familiar, and easy to administer. Behind the oaths stood a network of informants reporting violators to the ubiquitous committees of safety. New statutes defined treason, confiscated property from traitors, and set up inferior commissions and tribunals to ferret out suspicious behavior and punish disloyalty. The legislatures even passed bills of attainder, charging, trying, convicting, and ordering punishment for known Loyalists without allowing them a chance to defend themselves. Most state constitutions outlawed these quasi-judicial proceedings, which did not stop Georgia or Virginia from reinstituting them.

The legislatures' effort to protect the new states included direction of everyday military operations. The Continental Congress tried to manage its army by committee. State assemblies did the same with their militia. Some assemblies republicanized manuals of war detailing the conduct of officers and enlisted men and providing for uniforms, pay, and discharge. Legislatures also arranged for supply of the troops, heard disputes over rank and mistreatment, and even investigated the conduct of battles.

Energetic if makeshift arrangements could replace the officers of royal courts with good republican magistrates and on occasion prescribe intelligible rules of war, but the ultimate guarantor of the safety of republicanism was the refashioning of law itself. As the Virginia House of Delegates admitted in May 1776, "it will require considerable time to compile a body of laws suited to the circumstances of the country."[13] The reform of the laws was much debated, but little was accomplished. The House agreed that the statutes of England enacted prior to 1607, all general precepts of common law, and its own colonial statutes would remain in force until the laws could be revised. Many states followed the Virginia example. Virginia itself commissioned James Blair, Edmund Pendleton, and Jefferson, three of its leading lawyers, to republicanize its laws. Their suggestions on religious freedom and reform of the penal code were ultimately accepted. At their urging the state rid itself of primogeniture. Even the law of slavery was changed in 1782: men and women were allowed to manumit their slaves.

The second major area of revolutionary lawmaking was financial. As the mercantilists of the seventeenth century had discovered, the strength of the modern state rested upon its taxing power. For a confederation of states at war, the problem of public finance was critical. The states were sovereign and could tax their citizens. Congress, though it had charge of the war effort, could only requisition funds from the states or pay for its quartermasters' purchases with scrip. As the continental currency plummeted in value, the states and Congress borrowed to pay their bills. The new governments could hardly admit to bankruptcy and keep the allegiance of the farmers, merchants, and foreign suppliers necessary for the war effort.

One answer to the insatiable demand for income for the state was taxation in kind—a legal version of confiscation. For example, in October 1777, the Virginia House of Burgesses told magistrates to seize "for the use of the army any salt which they may discover in the possession of any person or persons within this commonwealth imported or purchased for sale."[14] In fact, local merchants had been buying salt before army purchasing agents could get to it, hoarding it to drive up the price and selling it to the army at exorbitant prices. Personal fortunes were made in this way, often with the connivance or aid of army staff officers. Such legislative regulation of the economy was not designed to promote efficiency or accumulation of capital, but to restrain private cupidity and peculation.

The revolutionary war complicated the normal budgetary functions of legislators. Not only did they have to forestall the corruptionists and speculators, the assemblymen had to pay for supplies, military service, and information about the enemy. Unable or unwilling to increase taxes (after all, that had been one cause of the rebellion), legislatures passed bond issues, printed money, confiscated and sold Loyalist land at auction, and ran lotteries. Increasingly, legislatures were forced to tax land and its products, a burden that fell disproportionately upon poorer farmers, including veterans, and their spouses. Resentment against this policy festered, and when creditors began to foreclose on bankrupt farmers after the war was over, the farmers resisted with force. Sharp affrays like Shays' rebellion in western Massachusetts (1786–87) occasioned much handwringing and soul-searching among leading politicians about the fate of the young republics and gave impetus to the federalist movement.

At the root of the politicians' fear was the conviction that the new American republics were not proof against the fate of their predecessors—the cycle of corruption, discontent, decay, and dissolution which enlightenment thinkers regarded as a law of nature. These fears gave rise to the third major subject of legislative activity: regulation of morals. The Revolution had begun with a *rage militaire* that was essentially religious, an outpouring of moral indignation at tyranny and violence. Moral indignation had not kept the army together (professionalism, training, and the bonds of honor and friendship did that), nor had it supplied the army when it starved in the winters of 1777–78 and 1779–80. Nevertheless, the legislators continued to regard the Revolution as a moral crusade. In this context, the state legislatures levied war on immorality, alcoholism, and debauchery as well as the troops of the king. The assemblies sought to regulate the supply and price of liquor, ban immoral conduct, and promote civic pride, subjects still high on many state governments' agendas.

Again the law was seen as well as heard. The source of law now appeared to the ordinary American, the consumer in the popular legal culture of that era, as an assemblage of men. Americans could see that law was not "discovered" in some arcane heaven of legal forms, but made by the representatives of the people. If not all the people were represented, at least all of them could watch as their assemblies and conventions gathered, sat on hard benches and chairs through hot days and fetid evenings, and argued about the common good. If the final version of the law made invidious distinctions between rich and poor, white and black, male and female, at least the servant and the laborer could see it all happening. In such a setting phrases such as "popular sovereignty" appeared to embody a significant piece of social reality.

This continuity between the first state constitutions and the first colonial efforts at self-governance grew out of the small scale and directness of lawmaking. When the planters of Virginia first gathered themselves into a House of Burgesses and the delegates to the Massachusetts General Court insisted on a code of laws, highly visible participatory lawmaking went hand in hand with reform of the laws. The framers of the first state constitutions carried on that tradition.

Public Law and Private Liberty

The new state constitutions diverged from the older colonial codes in one significant respect: a gradual but discernible separation of public and private law appeared. The doctrine that public law and private law were wholly distinct, the former the preserve of the legislature, the latter the concern of the courts, would not dominate American legal thinking until the middle of the nineteenth century, but the first steps toward that distinction were taken in the revolutionary era as the revolutionaries tried to justify themselves as defenders of "liberty" and "property."

The first colonists had believed that liberty lay in fulsome elucidation of all laws, because one's liberty was determined by one's status. A settler could claim certain "liberties"—the right to follow a trade or vote in an election—by law or custom. Good law enumerated such liberties so that everyone knew where he or she stood. In quite contrary fashion, the revolutionaries had come to think of liberty as an abstract quality of life, an area around the individual into which government might not penetrate. "Liberty" opposed arbitrary power; good law limited power in order to protect liberty.

Property for the first colonists had been inseparable from government: government granted land, conceded the privilege of erecting townships and parishes, and licensed activities of all kinds. Regulation of property was permissible because government also granted that bundle of relationships which allowed a person to enjoy one's land and chattels. For the revolutionaries, the independent ownership of land was the bedrock of republicanism. Both Jefferson and Adams proposed that men without land be given a freehold to prevent their corruption by the mighty. Servants would be too easily tempted or bullied by their masters to exercise independent judgment. Yeoman farmers could make up their own minds. Bit by bit, acquisitiveness itself became respectable, a legitimate form of personal liberty. A blossoming market economy, featuring competition and capital accumulation, remade the meaning of "self-interest." As Joyce Appleby has written, "the most subversive aspect of this imaginative model of the economy was the implication that government supervision of the economy was not only unwarranted, but ineffective, much like a statute against floods and earthquakes."[15]

In the continuing constitutional convention that was the revolutionary era, American political theorists began to assume that one of the purposes of government was to protect personal liberty and private property rather than to grant and define liberty and property. Beneath the altered assumptions of the lawyers was a deep shift in social attitudes. Republican constitutions had less to say about private law than the Massachusetts Body of Liberties of 1641 because the revolutionary lawgivers no longer believed that individual life must be lived in the confines of community. By 1776, the New England soldiers in the Continental army, some of them the great-, great-grandchildren of the Puritans of 1641, insisted upon their rights as individuals. Law conferred independence, not submissiveness to custom and tradition. For these patriots, private life and public service were separate spheres.

One by-product of the shift to new ideas of liberty and property was an admission that factionalism was inevitable in legislative bodies. Insecure in their moral preachments, beset by British troops and Loyalist enemies, cliques of revolutionaries wrangled over the shape of legislation. Faced with mounting debts, creditors tried to use the apparatus of lawmaking to collect from debtors. The economic partisanship took constitutional form, as western debtors demanded an equal share in governance with eastern creditors. The first American political parties emerged from these contests—not so well organized or so stable as parties today, but distinct nonetheless from the shifting, self-interested coalitions that dominated parliamentary and earlier American legislative politics. Constitution making thus overlapped and enfolded a struggle for who would rule at home.

Despite the internal struggles over the shape of constitutions and statutes, a regime of republican law gradually emerged in the United States. At its base was a system of representative government reserving to many but not all the people some measure of direct participation in their governance. Jefferson and John Adams still regarded the new system of states as a great experiment in self-government. The question lingered whether a revolutionary people could make fundamental law that would restrain the disorder that had fueled the Revolution but a generation before. With the benefit of hindsight, we can see that the framers' system of division of power among distinct branches of government and reservation of rights and liberties of individuals from public erosion (though the public interest could always be pleaded by officials who wished to alter the boundaries of individual liberty) has worked well. In large measure this achievement rested upon the revolutionaries' reintegration of formal law and the aspirations of a people.

CONCLUSION

Richard Bushman's superb *King and People in Provincial Massachusetts* (1985) identifies two overlapping sources of authority in prerevolutionary America: the king, whose moral legitimacy arose from his duty to protect the rights of the people, and the people themselves, loyal to the king until, quite abruptly, they rebelled and adopted republicanism. Bushman wrote that "the King and the people were not, however, separate or opposing moral centers. The rights and privileges of the people did not constitute a culture outside of monarchy; they were integral to it. Supposedly, royal power was devoted entirely to the well-being of the people. While they were defending popular rights, the popular party [in the colony] claimed perfect loyalty to the monarch, because the king himself was the foremost defender of those rights."[1] With the king repudiated, the revolutionary lawyers might well wonder if the popular will could be curbed.

It seems to me that Bushman's thesis can be extended into the revolutionary era if one substitutes "law" for "king." The substitution is not farfetched—after all, the common law was the king's law. His law and his courts protected the rights of the people more effectually than any other arm of his government. The Revolution exploded the relationship between crown and people but not that between law and people. As Thomas Jefferson insisted in the Declaration of Independence, the king had violated his own law, the law the colonies shared with England, in his haste to punish certain colonists. In Massachusetts, Bushman writes, "when the time came after independence to write a constitution for the state, it was a foregone conclusion that there would be no king, no independent fountain of power to appoint officials. There would just be one source of power, the people, and all of government would be dependent on them."[2]

When the Massachusetts Provincial Congress turned to the people of the towns for advice on a new constitution, there was great disagreement. A good lawyer, John Adams recognized that a people without law could not survive. The sovereign people must become the sovereign lawmaker, binding themselves and later generations. A truly republican system would allow latecomers to revise what their forebears had done, but only within the framework of known law which institution-alized popular will—to wit, law and people. Adams grasped that re-publicanism could only survive if the will of the people was channeled through law.

Adams had begun to elucidate what would later be known as the doctrine of "Rule of Law." In its fullest, modern form, Rule of Law is a very attractive ideal. Law is to be general, equally applied, feasible, predictable, stable, and clear to all. Lawmaking must be a public en-terprise, blind to special interests and powerful individuals, rational, and accessible. Rule of Law embodies the doctrines of due process and equal protection. Looking back, one can see that rudimentary prin-ciples of Rule of Law infused the first state and federal constitutions and the Bill of Rights. Even so, the language of the constitutions masked the political exclusion of certain groups. Indians, women, blacks, Catholics and Jews, and other disfavored groups did not gain equal rights with free white propertied males of the Protestant faith. Thus the framers' rules, the "original" frame of government, failed as Rule of Law. Only when the rules and the reality come together does Rule of Law become more than an apology or a masquerade. The re-integration of American law and people was incomplete in 1776, and in 1992 the promise of justice for all remains a bright, shining, but elusive goal.

NOTES

Preface

1. Alan Watson, *Failures of the Legal Imagination* (Philadelphia, 1988), 107.

Chapter One

1. Bernard, Bailyn, *The Peopling of British North America: An Introduction* (New York, 1986), 5.
2. John Baker's comment about Coke's writing style appears in Baker's *Introduction to English Legal History*, 2d ed. (London, 1979), 165.
3. Michael Dalton, *The Countrey Justice* (London, 1619), 7.
4. Winthrop's opinions on the unruly masses appeared in his "Common Grevances Groaninge for Reformation" (1624), a portion of which is quoted in Mark Bond-Webster, "John Winthrop's 'Christian Charity'" (Unpublished manuscript, 1990), 18.
5. The Gilbert patent appears in "The Letters Patent Granted by Her Majestie to Sir Humfrey Gilbert, Knight . . . 1578," in Richard Hakluyt, comp., *The Principal Navigations . . .*, ed. Irwin R. Blacker (New York, 1965), 211.
6. James I's address to Parliament is quoted in J. P. Kenyon, ed., *The Stuart Constitution* (Cambridge, 1966), 12–14.
7. Melvin B. Endy, Jr., "Just War, Holy War, and Millennialism in Revolutionary America," *William and Mary Quarterly*, 3d ser., 42 (1985): 8. Ordered by the appropriate religious authority, such a war was a "holy war." When the secular ruler initiated the war, it was a "just war."
8. Robert A. Williams, Jr., *The American Indian in Western Legal Thought: The Discourses of Conquest* (New York, 1990), 221.
9. The Virginia Charter of 1606 appears in William W. Hening, comp., *The Statutes at Large of Virginia* (Richmond, 1809–21), 1:64.
10. Stephen Saunders Webb, *The Governors-General: The English Army and the Definition of the Empire, 1569–1681* (Chapel Hill, 1979), 436.
11. The covenant agreed to by the emigrants from Dorchester was framed by John Higginson and entered into on August 6, 1630. I have quoted the text from Ola Elizabeth Winslow, *Meetinghouse Hill, 1630–1783*, 2d ed. (New York, 1972), 22.

12. Paul Boyer and Stephen Nissenbaum, *Salem Possessed: The Social Origins of Witchcraft* (Cambridge, Mass., 1974), 62.
13. Joseph H. Smith, ed., *Colonial Justice in Western Massachusetts (1639–1702): The Pynchon Court Record* (Cambridge, Mass., 1961), 89–91.

Chapter Two

1. Rhys Isaac, *The Transformation of Virginia, 1740–1790* (Chapel Hill, 1982), 92.
2. Wilfred J. Ritz, *Rewriting the History of the Judiciary Act of 1789*, ed. Wythe Holt and L. H. LaRue (Norman, Okla., 1990), 10.
3. Roger Williams, "To the General Court Delegates of Providence, May 16, 1647," in Glenn W. LaFantasie et al., eds., *The Correspondence of Roger Williams* (Hanover, N.H., 1988), 1:230.
4. William Penn, "Conditions or Concessions to the First Purchasers," July 11, 1681, in Richard S. Dunn and Mary Maples Dunn, eds., *The Papers of William Penn* (Philadelphia, 1982), 2:100.
5. Gloucester County Court of Common Pleas Minute Book No. 1, 1686–1703, Gloucester County Historical Society Library, Woodbury, N.J.
6. The description of the ill-fated practice of Thomas Lechford comes from Thomas G. Barnes, "Thomas Lechford and the Earliest Lawyering in Massachusetts, 1638–1641," in Daniel R. Coquillette, ed., *Law in Colonial Massachusetts, 1630–1800* (Boston, 1984), 3–38.
7. Robert Beverley, *The History and Present State of Virginia* [1705], ed. Louis B. Wright (Charlottesville, 1947), 255.
8. *Woodcocke v. Gregory* appears in Smith, ed., *Colonial Justice in Western Massachusetts*, 206–8.
9. Darrett B. Rutman and Anita H. Rutman, *A Place in Time: Middlesex County, Virginia, 1650–1750* (New York, 1984), 87.
10. Mattie E. E. Parker, ed., *North Carolina Higher Court Records, 1697–1701* (Raleigh, 1971), 78–83.
11. *Mead and Ingram v. Turner* appears in Zechariah Chafee, Jr., ed., *Records of the Suffolk County Court* (Boston, 1933), 1:36–43.
12. *Porter v. Steel* is reported in L. Kinvin Wroth and Hiller B. Zobel, eds., *The Legal Papers of John Adams* (Cambridge, Mass., 1965), 1:162–67.
13. The misconduct of North Carolina justices is noted in Donna J. Spindel, *Crime and Society in North Carolina* (Baton Rouge, 1989), 26–28. The manuring of the North Carolina bench is recounted in James P. Whittenburg, "Planters, Merchants, and Lawyers: Social Change and the Origins of the North Carolina Regulation," *William and Mary Quarterly*, 3d ser., 34 (1977): 237.
14. Pennsylvania Ordinance for Establishing of Courts (1707), Statutes at Large of Pennsylvania, 1:320. I have taken much of my discussion in this paragraph from Francis Fox's work in progress on the Pennsylvania prothonotaries and am grateful for his permission to preview it here.

15. Carol F. Karlsen, *The Devil in the Shape of a Woman: Witchcraft in Colonial New England* (New York, 1987), 235.
16. Samuel Sewall, "Bill Put up on Fast Day, January 14," [1697], in *The Diary of Samuel Sewall, 1674–1729*, ed. M. Halsey Thomas (New York, 1973), 1:367.
17. E. W. Ives, *The Common Lawyers of Pre-Reformation England* (Cambridge, 1983), 7.
18. Alan F. Day, *A Social Study of Lawyers in Maryland, 1660–1775* (New York, 1990), 4.
19. Gabriel Thomas, *Historical and Geographical Account of Pennsilvania* (London, 1698), ed. M. Monroe Aurand (Harrisburg, 1938), 20–21.
20. "An Act Relating to Attorneys" (1702), *The Acts and Resolves, Public and Private, of the Province of Massachusetts Bay* (Boston, 1869), 1:467.
21. "An Act of the Licensing of Attorneys" (1732), in Hening, comp., *Statutes at Large of Virginia*, 4:360–62. The 1643 act appears in Hening, 1:275.
22. James Oglethorpe to the Trustees of Georgia, December 1733, *Colonial Records of the State of Georgia*, ed. Kenneth Coleman and Milton Ready (Athens, Ga., 1982), 20:41; Samuel Eveleigh to James Oglethorpe, October 19, 1734, Ibid., 87.
23. Gary B. Nash, *The Urban Crucible: Social Change, Political Consciousness, and the Origins of the American Revolution* (Cambridge, Mass., 1979), 32.
24. David Lovejoy, *The Glorious Revolution in America* (New York, 1972), 271.
25. *An Essay upon the Government of the English Plantations on the Continent of America* [1701], ed. Louis B. Wright (San Marino, Calif., 1945), 23.

Chapter Three

1. Richard Posner, *The Federal Courts: Crisis and Reform* (Cambridge, Mass., 1985), 7.
2. David Thomas Konig, *Law and Society in Puritan Massachusetts, Essex County, 1629–1692* (Chapel Hill, 1979), 108.
3. Both cases were played out on December 2, 1695, and June 1, 1696, in the Gloucester County Court of Common Pleas. Gloucester County Court of Common Pleas Minute Book No. 1, 161–71; Gloucester County Historical Society Library, Woodbury, N.J. The "more ominous" was already in the wings: the Harrisons sought an indictment against the Eglingtons for receiving a "stolen" apple pie. The justices also imposed an end to the accusation of theft. See Attestation of Sarah Harrison, October 28, 1695, Transcriptions of the . . . Documents of Old Gloucester . . . 1:28; Gloucester County Historical Society Library.
4. William McEnery Offutt, Jr., "Law and Social Cohesion in a Plural Society: The Delaware Valley, 1680–1710" (Ph.D. diss., The Johns Hopkins University, 1987), 57, 81, 84, 176–79.

5. Thomas Purvis, *Proprietors, Patronage, and Paper Money: Legislative Politics in New Jersey, 1703–1776* (New Brunswick, N.J., 1986), 208.
6. Adams, Diary entry for June 19, 1760, in *The Diary and Autobiography of John Adams*, ed. L. H. Butterfield (New York, 1964), 1:136–37.
7. Bruce Mann, *Neighbors and Strangers: Law and Community in Early Connecticut* (Chapel Hill, 1987), 9–10, 42–43, 167–68.
8. Cornelia Hughes Dayton, "Men, Women, and Credit in Commercializing Eighteenth-Century New England" (Paper presented at the Clark Library Seminar, April 20, 1990), 22.
9. Christine Heyrman, *Commerce and Culture: The Maritime Communities of Colonial Massachusetts, 1690–1750* (New York, 1984), 74.
10. Barbara A. Black, "Nathaniel Byfield, 1653–1733," in Coquillette, ed., *Law in Colonial Massachusetts*, 85.
11. Data from the *Acts and Resolves . . . of Massachusetts Bay* (Boston, 1869), 1:460–554 and 4:5–436, cited in Alison Gilbert Olson, "The 'Rise' of Three Colonial Legislatures in the Eighteenth Century: Virginia, Massachusetts, and Pennsylvania" (Paper presented to the Philadelphia Center for Early American Studies, October 5, 1990), 35.
12. Jefferson's observations of the Maryland assembly were contained in a letter to John Gage written on May 25, 1766. It is reproduced in Wilbur Samuel Howell, ed., *The Papers of Thomas Jefferson*, 2d ser., *Jefferson's Parliamentary Writings* (Princeton, 1988), 3–4.

Chapter Four

1. Gloucester County Court of Common Pleas Minute Book No. 3 (October 6, 1708), 355; Gloucester County Historical Society Library, Woodbury, N.J.
2. Adams' satire of legal education appears in *Diary and Autobiography of John Adams*, ed. Butterfield, 3:272–73.
3. William Livingston, *The Independent Reflector*, No. XXVIII (June 7, 1753), in Milton Klein, ed., *The Independent Reflector* (Cambridge, Mass., 1963), 254.
4. John M. Murrin, "The Legal Transformation: The Bench and Bar of Eighteenth-Century Massachusetts," in Stanley N. Katz, ed., *Colonial America: Essays in Politics and Social Development* (Boston, 1971), 442.
5. The story of Abel Pooley appears in Day, *A Social Study of Lawyers in Maryland*, 21.
6. Livingston's contributions to the genre of criticism of law appear in William Livingston, *The Art of Pleading* (New York, 1751), quoted in Stephen Botein, *Early American Law and Society* (New York, 1983), 118.
7. Hamilton's remark is reported in Julius Goebel, Jr., et al., eds., *Law Practice of Alexander Hamilton* (New York, 1964–84), 1:52.
8. Lord Bellomont to the Lords of Trade [Westminster, England], Novem-

ber 28, 1700, *Documents Relating to the Colonial History of the State of New York*, ed. E. B. O'Callahan (Albany, 1854), 4:791.

9. Lawrence Friedman, *A History of American Law*, 2d ed. (New York, 1985), 62.

10. Alan Taylor, "'A Kind of Warr': The Contest for Land on the Northeastern Frontier, 1750–1820," *William and Mary Quarterly*, 3d ser., 46 (1989): 26.

11. Purchase Brown's troubles are recounted in Robert A. Gross, *The Minutemen and Their World* (New York, 1976), 85.

12. Susan Staves, *Married Women's Separate Property in England, 1660–1833* (Cambridge, Mass., 1990), 229.

13. Nancy F. Cott, "Divorce and the Changing Status of Women in Eighteenth-Century Massachusetts," *William and Mary Quarterly*, 3d ser., 33 (1976): 613.

14. Cornelia Hughes Dayton, "Women before the Bar: Gender, Law, and Society in Connecticut, 1710–1790" (Ph.D. diss., Princeton University, 1986), 164.

15. Thomas Smith, *De Republica Anglorum: A Discourse on the Commonwealth of England*, ed. Mary Dewar (Cambridge, 1982), 114.

16. The 40-percent acquittal figure comes from James Cockburn, "Introduction," *Calendar of Assize Records, Home Circuit Indictments, Elizabeth I and James I* (London, 1985), 113.

17. Stephan Landesman, "The Rise of the Contentious Spirit: Adversary Procedure in Eighteenth-Century England," *Cornell Law Review* 75 (1990): 562.

18. Stanley N. Katz, "Introduction," in Katz, ed., *A Brief Narrative of the Case and Trial of John Peter Zenger, by James Alexander* (Cambridge, Mass., 1963), 96.

19. The selection from the diary of Waitstill Avery appears in Spindel, *Crime and Society in North Carolina*, 39.

20. David H. Flaherty, "Criminal Practice in Provincial Massachusetts," in Coquillette, ed., *Law in Colonial Massachusetts*, 240–41.

21. William Nelson, "The Eighteenth-Century Background of John Marshall's Constitutional Jurisprudence," *Michigan Law Review* 76 (1978): 904.

22. Adams, Diary Note on the Right of Juries, February 12, 1771, prepared for delivery at the trial, on appeal, of *Longman v. Mein*, at the Superior Court of Judicature of Massachusetts, in Wroth and Zobel, eds., *Legal Papers of John Adams*, 1:230.

23. N. E. H. Hull, *Female Felons: Women and Serious Crime in Colonial Massachusetts* (Urbana, Ill., 1987), 122–23.

24. A. Roger Ekirch, *Bound for America: The Transportation of British Convicts to the Colonies, 1718–1775* (Oxford, 1987), 176–77.

25. Edmund S. Morgan, *American Slavery, American Freedom* (New York, 1975), 310.

26. William Lee's case is traced in Peter Charles Hoffer and William B. Scott,

eds., *Criminal Proceedings in Colonial Virginia: The Richmond County Record . . . 1711–1754* (Washington, D.C., and Athens, Ga., 1984), 218–19.

27. Matthew Hardy's case is mentioned in Spindel, *Crime and Society in North Carolina*, 48.

28. Winthrop Jordan, *White over Black* (Chapel Hill, 1968), 108.

29. Daniel Horsmanden, *The New York Conspiracy* [1744], ed. Thomas J. Davis (New York, 1971), 39.

30. Thomas Jefferson, ed., *Reports of Cases Determined in the General Court of Virginia* (Richmond, 1829), 90–95.

Chapter Five

1. Blackstone's thoughts on law and liberty appear in Gareth Jones, ed., *The Sovereignty of the Law, Selections from Blackstone's Commentaries on the Laws of England* (Toronto, 1973), 4–5. The lecture was the very first Vinerian lecture at Oxford, given on October 25, 1758.

2. John Phillip Reid, *The Concept of Representation in the Age of the American Revolution* (Chicago, 1989), 85.

3. Ibid., 30.

4. Josiah Quincy, Jr., to the Jury, *The Trial of the British Soldiers . . .*, (Boston, 1807) 41.

5. Hutchinson's charge to the grand jury is recorded in Samuel Quincy, ed., *Reports of Cases Argued before the Superior Court of Judicature . . . by Josiah Quincy* (Boston, 1856), 268.

6. John Dickinson, "Letters from a Farmer in Pennsylvania to the Inhabitants of the British Colonies" [1768], in Merrill Jensen, ed., *Tracts of the American Revolution, 1763–1776* (Indianapolis, 1967), 129, 133, 137, 152.

7. Wilson's unpublished address appears in James Wilson, "Considerations on Parliament" [1768], in Robert McCloskey, ed., *Works of James Wilson* (Cambridge, Mass., 1967), 2:734, 735.

8. Ibid.

9. Wilson's speech to the Pennsylvania assembly is reprinted in McCloskey, ed., *Works of Wilson*, 2:747–58.

10. The Trowbridge Memorandum is printed in Peter Charles Hoffer and N. E. H. Hull, *Impeachment in America, 1635–1805* (New Haven, 1984), 52–53.

11. Adams' correspondence with Mason is reproduced in Robert J. Taylor et al., eds., *The Papers of John Adams* (Cambridge, Mass., 1979–), 4:373–75, 391–93, 447–49, and 479–81.

12. John Adams, "Thoughts on Government," in Taylor et al., eds., *Papers of John Adams*, 4:86, 87, 91.

13. Hening, comp., *Statutes at Large of Virginia*, 9:126 (1776).

14. Ibid., 381 (1777).

15. Joyce Appleby, *Capitalism and a New Social Order: The Republican Vision of the 1790s* (New York, 1984), 34.

Conclusion

1. Richard Bushman, *King and People in Provincial Massachusetts* (Chapel Hill, 1985), 5.
2. Ibid., 229.

A BIBLIOGRAPHIC ESSAY

There is a paradox at the heart of legal history: law touches everyone; law reflects everyday life; but law is also capable of great complexity. It is not easy to write legal history that is both "correct" in a technical sense and true to the experience of lay people who "went to law" to maintain their dignity or recover their rights. This book offers my own thinking about the central issues in our first experience with law, but if I have my own perspective, it is because I was able to stand on the shoulders of many other scholars. I have tried to give credit to all of them, but this bibliography is far from exhaustive.

The reader will find excellent bibliographies containing other sources in Stephen Botein, *Early American Law and Society* (New York, 1983); George Dargo, *Law in the New Republic: Private Law and Public Estate* (New York, 1983); Douglas Greenberg, *Crime and Law Enforcement in the Colony of New York, 1691–1776* (Ithaca, N.Y., 1976); Herbert A. Johnson, *Essays on New York Colonial Legal History* (Westport, Conn., 1981); David Thomas Konig, *Law and Society in Puritan Massachusetts, Essex County, 1629–1692* (Chapel Hill, 1979); and J. M. Sosin, *The Aristocracy of the Long Robe: The Origin of Judicial Review in America* (New York, 1989).

For early printed sources, one should consult Eldon R. James, "A List of Legal Treatises Printed in the British Colonies and the American States Before 1801," *Harvard Legal Essays* (Cambridge, Mass., 1934), 159–211, and Wilfred J. Ritz, comp., *American Judicial Proceedings First Printed before 1801* (Westport, Conn., 1984).

Introduction

The originators of the inate, genetic approach to legal history were the common-law judges themselves. They wrote the first histories of the law, garlanded with their own commentaries on important cases. Such influential works as Edward Coke's *Institutes of the Laws of England* (London, 1628–44), Matthew Hale's *History of the Common Law* (London, 1713), and William Blackstone's *Commentaries on the Laws of England* (Oxford, 1765–69) defended the common law while recounting its history. A much more sophisticated version of this tradition was continued by scholars such as Frederick Pollock and Frederic W. Maitland, *History of English Law before the Time of Edward I* (Cambridge, 1898); William Holdsworth, *History of English Law* (London, 1903–66), 16 vols.; Theodore F. C. Plucknett, *A Concise History of English Law*, 5th ed.

(Boston, 1956); and, most recently, John H. Baker's *Introduction to English Legal History*, 2d ed. (London, 1979), to which I am particularly indebted. A third edition of Baker's work is in press as I write.

Not all English legal scholars hewed to the line laid down by Coke and Hale. Some have approached law as the product of a dominant class, for example, Douglas Hay et al., *Albion's Fatal Tree: Crime and Society in Eighteenth-Century England* (New York, 1975), and Edward P. Thompson, *Whigs and Hunters: The Origins of the Black Act* (New York, 1975).

In the United States, the autonomous approach to legal history was early defended by judges greatly influenced by the English judicial tradition. Typically, in the first half of the nineteenth century, James Kent's four volumes of *Commentaries on American Law* (New York, 1827–30), 1:312, regarded the growth of the common law as a manifestation of natural law. In our own century, law professors Julius Goebel, Jr., and Joseph H. Smith were the foremost expositors of the internalist tradition.

In opposition to Kent's views, nineteenth-century law reformers such as William Sampson and Robert Rantoul, Jr., argued that American law ought to be different from English law because American history was different from English history. These legal reformers were the first proponents of a "law and society" view of legal history. Today, scholars Lawrence Friedman, Kermit L. Hall, Hendrik Hartog, George L. Haskins, Morton Horwitz, James Willard Hurst, William E. Nelson, Harry Schieber, and G. Edward White, among others, press for a study of law in the context of social thought and action.

My concept of a legal system and a legal culture was greatly influenced by Lawrence Friedman's *Law and Society: An Introduction* (Englewood Cliffs, N.J., 1977). The idea of law as a discourse, a language, I have adapted from J. G. A. Pocock's essay "The State of the Art," in Pocock, *Virtue, Commerce, and History* (Cambridge, 1985), 14–17, and David Hollinger's essay "Historians and the Discourse of Intellectuals," in his *In the American Province: Studies in the History and Historiography of Ideas*, 2d ed. (Baltimore, 1985), 130–51. The idea that a community of professional lawyers and jurists shared a language and discoursed in it over the course of generations seems to me to fit legal history.

There is no single, definitive account of law in early America, but as Lawrence Friedman has said in his eminently readable *History of American Law*, 2d ed. (New York, 1985), 15, the field is well on its way to "maturity." Friedman's chapters on colonial law are illuminating and concise, reflecting his commitment to law and society. Sosin's *Aristocracy of the Long Robe* traces the struggle between legislative and judicial bodies for the last word on law. Kermit L. Hall has edited a series of volumes of articles on American legal history for Garland Publishers entitled *U.S. Constitutional and Legal History* (New York, 1987), some of which cover the colonial period, and his *Magic Mirror: Law in American History* (New York, 1989) has two chapters on the prerevolutionary era. Botein's well-crafted essay and collection of documents *Early American Law and Society* is still available. The essays collected in David H. Flaherty's *Essays in the History of Early American Law* (Chapel Hill,

1969) are now dated but still full of energy. They reflect the conflict between
the internalist and externalist schools in the first half of the twentieth century.
Richard Morris's *Studies in the History of American Law, with Special Reference to the Seventeenth and Eighteenth Centuries* [1930], 2d ed. (New York,
1959), never received the credit a truly pioneering study is due, and now its
conclusions are much controverted.

Chapter One

The transmission of signs and signals like the rules of law is a complex process.
Scholars have offered four scenarios for reception of English law in the colonies. The first is that the whole of the common law was received and was in
force from the time of settlement. This internalist theory was favored by conservative judges and scholars in the nineteenth century but has few adherents
today.

A second, externalist theory of reception gained adherents at the turn of the
century. Paul S. Reinsch, a University of Wisconsin professor of political science influenced by historian Frederick Jackson Turner's "frontier theory" of
American history (also fashioned at the University of Wisconsin), argued that
American law was wholly indigenous. The forms and language may have resembled English law, but the administration of the law—the law in fact—was
American. What was more, it was frontier law—more individualistic, egalitarian, and progressive than English law. See Reinsch, "The English Common
Law in the Early American Colonies," *Select Essays in Anglo-American Legal
History* (Boston, 1907), 1:367–79. The "frontier theory" of law no longer has a
large following among scholars.

In later years, two more theories issued from the law schools, again taking
opposite sides in the internalist-externalist debate. In the first, Julius Goebel,
Jr., a legal historian at Columbia Law School and the author of many books
on English law, argued that the Pilgrims brought with them an imperfectly
realized but pervasive attachment to manorial law modified slightly by their
covenant religion. Goebel argued that the Pilgrims used the model of "borough
franchises," grants by kings to local communities, to lay out their towns, divide
the land, prosecute crime, and run their government. See Goebel, "King's Law
and Local Custom in Seventeenth-Century New England," *Columbia Law Review* 31 (1931): 416–48. Goebel's view of transmission and his internalist approach to legal history were adopted by Joseph H. Smith. See Smith, *The English Legal System: Carryover to the Colonies* (Los Angeles, 1975), and Smith,
Appeals to the Privy Council from the American Plantations (New York,
1950).

More recently, historian David Grayson Allen has unearthed the close connection between the "courts baron and leet" of eastern Yorkshire and the by-
laws of the Massachusetts town of Rowley, nestled on the coast between Boston and Salem. The open-field, communal agriculture of the north of England
required manorial supervision, and the emigrants brought with them the ma-

norial system used to manage disputes among the farmers and weavers of their late home. The Pilgrims had come from the same area of England. See Allen, *In English Ways: The Movement of Societies and the Transferral of English Local Law and Custom to Massachusetts Bay in the Seventeenth Century* (Chapel Hill, 1982).

Pennsylvania Law School's George Haskins looked in a different place for the boundaries of the legal system. In "Law and Colonial Society," an *American Quarterly* article published in 1957, Haskins wrote: "It is when we turn to particular rules of law as revealed in the court records, and especially to the innovations introduced by the colonists, that we find reflected most clearly the social organization of the colony, its general purposes and aims, and the pressures for change and adaptation resulting from political and economic needs." For Haskins, the law was part of the larger social fabric. Mark DeWolfe Howe, "The Sources and Nature of Law in Colonial Massachusetts," in George Athan Billias, ed., *Law and Authority in Colonial America* (Barré, Mass., 1965), 1–15, and Bradley Chapin, *Criminal Justice in Colonial America, 1606–1660* (Athens, Ga., 1983), adopted the Haskins thesis.

Great writers have always been aware of the importance of telling a story through the eyes of its participants—literally recounting what they saw and heard. The greatest visual depiction of the civil side of the law comes from Charles Dickens' pen. Nothing matches his portrait of chancery in the opening pages of *Bleak House* (London, 1853): "Well may the court be dim, with wasting candles here and there, well may the fog hang heavy in it, as if it would never get out; well may the stained glass windows lose their color, and admit no light of day into the place, well may the uninitiated from the streets, who peep in through the glass panes in the door, be deterred from entrance by its owlish aspect, and by the drawl languidly echoing to the roof from the padded dais where the Lord High Chancellor looks into the lantern that has no light in it, and where the attendant wigs are all stuck in a fog-bank!" (Modern Library Edition, New York, 1985), 6. Few historians write as well as Dickens, but I have not found a rival to T. P. S. Woods' graphic depiction of an early seventeenth-century assize judge's travails in *Prelude to Civil War, 1642: Mr. Justice Malet and the Kentish Petitions* (London, 1980).

On the common-law idea of precedent, an intriguing recent essay is Melvin Aron Eisenberg, *The Nature of the Common Law* (Cambridge, Mass., 1988). For a general survey of the English law, courts, and legal process, one can rely upon Baker's *Introduction to English Legal History* and S. F. C. Milsom, *Historical Foundations of the Common Law*, 2d ed. (London, 1981). Holdsworth's mammoth *History of English Law* is still invaluable. Coke listed and described the courts in *The Fourth Part of the Institutes . . .* (London, 1644). Material on Coke came from his own works, Catherine Drinker Bowen's lively *The Lion and the Throne: The Life and Time of Sir Edward Coke* (Boston, 1957), and Christopher Hill's far less admiring "Sir Edward Coke—Myth-Maker," in *Intellectual Origins of the English Revolution* (Oxford, 1965), 225–65.

Robert C. Palmer's *County Courts of Medieval England, 1150–1350* (Princeton, 1982) is a controversial and superbly argued account of the growing authority of the king's courts. James Cockburn's *History of the English Assizes, 1558–1714* (Cambridge, 1972) and his editions of the assize records for the home circuit describe the rise and functioning of the royal courts of criminal justice. One should also read John H. Langbein's *Prosecuting Crime in the Renaissance* (Cambridge, Mass., 1974).

A sharply focused picture of local justice appears in Buchanan Sharp's *In Contempt of All Authority: Rural Artisans and Riot in the West of England, 1586–1660* (Berkeley, 1980) and the marvelous essays in John Brewer and John Styles' *An Ungovernable People: The English and Their Law in the Seventeenth and Eighteenth Centuries* (New Brunswick, N.J., 1980), in particular John Walter's "Grain Riots and Popular Attitudes toward the Law" and Keith Wrightson's "Two Concepts of Order: Justices, Constables, and Jurymen in Seventeenth-Century England," as well as Wrightson and David Levine's *Poverty and Piety in an English Village, Terling, 1525–1700* (New York, 1979).

The social unrest at the heart of the late Elizabethan and early Stuart period led to increased rates of crime and accusations of crime. See, generally, James A. Sharpe, *Crime in Early Modern England, 1550–1750* (London, 1984). On the connection between social disorder and crime see Cynthia Herrup, *The Common Peace: Participation and the Criminal Law in Seventeenth-Century England* (Cambridge, 1987); A. D. J. Macfarlane, *Witchcraft in Tudor and Stuart England* (New York, 1970); and Peter Charles Hoffer and N. E. H. Hull, *Murdering Mothers: Infanticide in England and New England, 1558–1803* (New York, 1981). On the general climate of the age, see Carl Bridenbaugh, *Vexed and Troubled Englishmen, 1590–1642*, rev. ed. (New York, 1976).

My account of the crisis of early seventeenth-century England follows Lawrence Stone's conclusion that there were "massive shifts in world views and value systems that occurred in England over a period of some three hundred years, from 1500 to 1800" (*The Family, Sex, and Marriage in England, 1500–1800*, abridged ed. [New York, 1979], 21). One cannot, however, ignore Peter Laslett's nostalgic vision in *The World We Have Lost: England before the Industrial Age* (New York, 1965), 21: "Time was when the whole of life went forward in the family, in a circle of loved, familiar faces, known and fondled objects, all to human size. That time has gone for ever. It makes us very different from our ancestors." Stone sees an early Stuart England undergoing modernization; Laslett, an England nestling in custom until rudely awakened by the sound of machinery later in the next century.

The study of the sea dogs is best told in their own words, collected by Richard Hakluyt, in his *Principal Navigations, Voyages, Traffiques, and Discoveries of the English Nation* (London, 1600). The colorful world of Elizabethan empire is captured in A. L. Rowse, *The Elizabethan Age* (London, 1971), and Howard Mumford Jones, *O Strange New World, American Culture: The Formative Years* (New York, 1952).

The standard account of the founding of the colonies remains Charles McLean Andrews, *The Colonial Period of American History*, 4 vols. (New Haven, 1923–36), though it must now be supplemented by Stephen Saunders Webb, *The Governors-General: The English Army and the Definition of the Empire,*

1569–1681 (Chapel Hill, 1979). Both Andrews and Webb built upon the work of their predecessors and contemporaries. Articles by these early scholars, including Herbert Levi Osgood, Edward Potts Cheyney, Mary P. Clarke, and Curtis Nettels, among others, are collected in Peter Charles Hoffer, ed., *The Context of Colonization* and *An Empire Takes Shape*, Vols. 1 and 3 of *Early American History* (New York, 1989).

The commercial revolution of which England's colonial enterprise was a part is traced in Fernand Braudel, *The Wheels of Commerce, Civilization, and Capitalism, Fifteenth to Eighteenth Century, Vol. 2*, Eng. tr. (New York, 1982), and Theodore K. Rabb, *Enterprise and Empire: Merchant and Gentry Investment in the Expansion of England, 1575–1630* (Cambridge, Mass., 1967). Earlier classics on the interplay of religion and capitalism are Max Weber, *The Protestant Ethic and the Spirit of Capitalism* (London, 1930), and R. H. Tawney's spirited reply, *Religion and the Rise of Capitalism* (New York, 1954). Similar longing for national wealth, filtered through different social structures and religious doctrines, had led Spain and France to empire building in the New World. See Charles Gibson, *Spain in America* (New York, 1966), and W. J. Eccles, *France in America* (New York, 1972).

John Smith's story is well told in Alden T. Vaughan, *American Genesis: Captain John Smith and the Founding of Virginia* (Boston, 1975). John Smith's *History of Virginia*, an advertisement for himself which did not get him the job he wanted but did publicize the colony, has been superbly edited by Philip L. Barbour in *The Complete Works of Captain John Smith, 1580–1631* (Chapel Hill, 1986). Anyone interested in the ironies of early Virginia history and law should read Edmund S. Morgan, *American Slavery, American Freedom: The Ordeal of Colonial Virginia* (New York, 1975); David Thomas Konig, "'Dale's Laws' and the Non–Common Law Origins of Criminal Justice in Virginia," *American Journal of Legal History* 24 (1982): 354–75; and Konig, "Colonization and the Common Law in Ireland and Virginia, 1569–1634," in James Henretta et al., eds., *The Transformation of Early American History: Society, Authority, and Ideology* (New York, 1991), 70–92. The social context of early Virginia law is traced in the essays in Thad W. Tate and David L. Ammerman, eds., *The Chesapeake in the Seventeenth Century: Essays on Anglo-American Society* (Chapel Hill, 1979), and Darrett B. Rutman and Anita H. Rutman, *A Place in Time: Middlesex County, Virginia, 1650–1750* (New York, 1984). The material on John Selden comes from David S. Berkowitz, *John Selden's Formative Years* (Washington, D.C., 1988).

Allen's *In English Ways* argues that the settlers of New England not only tried to re-create traditional forms of land use and town government, but that this persistence itself persisted through two generations. Though differing somewhat in thesis from Allen, Philip J. Greven, *Four Generations: Population, Land, and Family in Colonial Andover, Massachusetts* (Ithaca, N.Y., 1970); Kenneth Lockridge, *A New England Town, the First Hundred Years, Dedham, Massachusetts, 1636–1736* (New York, 1970); Sumner Chilton Powell, *Puritan Village: The Formation of a New England Town* (Middletown, Conn., 1963); Darrett B. Rutman, *Winthrop's Boston: A Portrait of a Puritan Town,*

1630–1649 (Chapel Hill, 1965); and Michael Zuckerman, *Peaceable Kingdoms: New England Towns in the Eighteenth Century* (New York, 1970), are equally valuable and readable precursors. The notion that these first towns were peaceable in their domestic affairs is questioned in Stephen Innes, *Labor in a New Land: Economy and Society in Seventeenth-Century Springfield* (Princeton, 1983).

On law reform and the Puritans, see G. B. Warden, "Law Reform in England and New England, 1620 to 1660," *William and Mary Quarterly*, 3d ser., 35 (1978): 668–90; Stuart E. Prall, *The Agitation for Law Reform during the Puritan Revolution, 1640–1660* (The Hague, 1966); Donald Veall, *The Popular Movement for Law Reform, 1640–1660* (Oxford, 1970); C. W. Brooks, *Pettifoggers and vipers of the Commonwealth: The 'lower branch' of the legal profession in early modern England* (Cambridge, 1986); and Nancy L. Matthews, *William Sheppard, Cromwell's Law Reformer* (Cambridge, 1984).

On the interplay of Puritanism and law in the early history of Massachusetts, see George L. Haskins, *Law and Authority in Early Massachusetts: A Study in Tradition and Design* (New York, 1960); Edmond S. Morgan, *The Puritan Dilemma: The Story of John Winthrop* (Boston, 1958); Robert Middlekauff, *The Mathers: Three Generations of Puritan Intellectuals, 1596–1728* (New York, 1971); T. H. Breen, *The Good Ruler: A Study of Puritan Political Ideas in New England, 1630–1730* (New Haven, 1970); and Konig, *Law and Society in Puritan Massachusetts*. The role of the General Court and the Assistants has been thoroughly discussed in Barbara A. Black, "The Judicial Power and the General Court in Early Massachusetts" (Ph.D. diss., Yale University, 1975). The discretion of magistrates under the "Liberties" is treated in Mark D. Cahn, "Punishment, Discretion, and the Codification of Prescribed Penalties in Colonial Massachusetts," *American Journal of Legal History* 33 (1989): 101–36.

On the theory of deviance and the use of criminal law as a boundary marker, see Kai T. Erikson, *Wayward Puritans: A Study in the Sociology of Deviance* (New York, 1966), and John P. Demos, *Entertaining Satan: Witchcraft and the Culture of Early New England* (New York, 1982).

On local justice in early Massachusetts, see David H. Flaherty, "Law and the Enforcement of Morals in Early America," in *Perspectives in American History* 5 (1971): 203–56; Eli Faber, "Puritan Criminals: The Economic, Social, and Intellectual Background to Crime in Seventeenth-Century Massachusetts," *Perspectives in American History* 11 (1978): 81–144; Joseph H. Smith, ed., *Colonial Justice in Western Massachusetts (1639–1702): The Pynchon Court Record* (Cambridge, Mass., 1961); Lyle Koehler, *A Search for Power: The "Weaker" Sex in Seventeenth-Century New England* (Urbana, Ill., 1980); and Roger Thompson, *Sex in Middlesex: Popular Mores in a Massachusetts County, 1649–1699* (Amherst, Mass., 1986).

On the Puritans and the Indians, see James Axtell, *The Invasion Within: The Contest of Cultures in Colonial North America* (New York, 1985); Francis Jennings, *The Invasion of America: Indians, Colonialism, and the Cant of Conquest* (Chapel Hill, 1975); and Alden T. Vaughan, *New England Frontier: Puri-*

tans and Indians, 1620–1675, rev. ed. (New York, 1979). Older essays on legal relations between settlers and Indians include Wilcomb E. Washburn, "The Moral and Legal Justification for Dispossessing the Indians," in James Morton Smith, ed., *Seventeenth-Century America: Essays in Colonial History* (Chapel Hill, 1959), 15–32, and Anthony F. C. Wallace, "Political Organization and Land Tenure among the Northern Indians, 1600–1830," *Southwestern Journal of Anthropology* 13 (1957): 301–21. The Indians of Virginia fared even worse than the Indians of New England. See Alden T. Vaughan, "'Expulsion of the Salvages': English Policy and the Virginia Massacre of 1622," *William and Mary Quarterly*, 3d ser., 35 (1978): 57–84.

The differences between the first northern and southern mainland colonies are traced in Jack P. Greene, *Pursuits of Happiness: The Social Development of Early Modern British Colonies and the Formation of American Culture* (Chapel Hill, 1988).

Chapter Two

On colonial visions of the land, see William Cronon's *Changes in the Land: Indians, Colonists, and the Ecology of New England* (New York, 1983); Rhys Isaac, *The Transformation of Virginia, 1740–1790* (Chapel Hill, 1982); and A. G. Roeber's depiction of "court day" in Virginia, in "Authority, Law, and Custom: The Rituals of Court Day in Tidewater Virginia, 1720 to 1750," *William and Mary Quarterly*, 3d ser., 37 (1980): 29–52.

I have chosen to diminish intercolonial divergences by emphasizing common trends in the colonies, in the process magnifying the differences between the colonies and England. On South Carolina law, see Herbert Johnson, ed., *South Carolina Legal History* (Spartanburg, S.C., 1980), and Anne King Gregorie, ed., *Records of the Court of Chancery of South Carolina, 1671–1776* (Washington, D.C., 1950). On New Haven, see Gail Sussman Marcus, "'Due Execution of the Generall Rules of Righteousnesse': Criminal Procedure in New Haven Town and Colony," in David D. Hall et al., eds., *Saints and Revolutionaries: Essays on Early American History* (New York, 1984), 99–137. On Rhode Island, see Chapin, *Criminal Justice*, which regards the law of the colony as influenced by (if not imitative of) common law, and G. B. Warden, "The Rhode Island Civil Code of 1647," in Hall, et al., ed., *Saints and Revolutionaries*, 138–51, which finds that the common-law citations in the code were no more than window dressing.

On equity in the colonies, see Peter Charles Hoffer, *The Law's Conscience: Equitable Constitutionalism in America* (Chapel Hill, 1990), Chap. 3, and Stanley N. Katz, "The Politics of Law in Colonial America: Controversies over Chancery Courts and Equity Law in the Eighteenth Century," *Perspectives in American History* 5 (1971): 257–86.

New York law is discussed in Judith A. Gilbert, "History of the Corporation Counsel of New York City" (Ph.D. diss. forthcoming from the Graduate Center of the City University of New York); Herbert A. Johnson, *Essays on New York Colonial Legal History* (Westport, Conn., 1981); Eben Moglen, "Settling the Law: Legal Development in Colonial New York" (Ph.D. diss., Yale University, 1992); Paul M. Hamlin and Charles E. Baker, eds., *Supreme Court of Judicature of the Province of New York, 1691–1704*, 2 vols. (New York, 1959); and Deborah A. Rosen, "The Supreme Court of Judicature of Colonial New York: Civil Practice in Transition, 1691–1760," *Law and History Review* 5 (1987): 213–48.

The Pennsylvania exception is discussed in Richard S. Dunn and Mary Maples Dunn, eds., *The World of William Penn* (Philadelphia, 1986), and Joseph E. Illick, *Colonial Pennsylvania: A History* (New York, 1976). Gary B. Nash has written about the first settlers and their conduct in *Quakers and Politics: Pennsylvania, 1681–1726* (Princeton, 1968). The Penn papers have been edited by Richard S. Dunn and others in five volumes of *The Papers of William Penn* (Philadelphia, 1981–87). Illick's book has a good bibliography for material to 1976. The essays in *The World of William Penn* carry the story through the next decade.

On New Jersey, see Preston W. Edsall, ed., *Journal of the Courts of Common Right and Chancery of East New Jersey, 1683–1702* (Philadelphia, 1937); H. Clay Reed and George L. Miller, eds., *The Burlington Court Book: A Record of Equity Jurisprudence in West New Jersey, 1680–1709* (Washington, D.C., 1944); and Richard S. Fields, "The Provincial Courts of New Jersey," *Collections of the New Jersey Historical Society* 9 (1849).

On lay judges in Massachusetts, see George L. Haskins, "Lay Judges: Magistrates and Justices in Early Massachusetts," and Russell K. Osgood, "John Clark, Esq., Justice of the Peace, 1667–1728," in Daniel R. Coquillette, ed., *Law in Colonial Massachusetts, 1630–1800* (Boston, 1984), 39–56 and 107–52. Samuel Sewall's career is traced in David H. Flaherty, "Chief Justice Samuel Sewall, 1692–1728," in William Pencak and Wythe Holt, Jr., eds., *The Law in America, 1607–1861* (New York, 1989), 114–54.

The witchcraft cases are explored in Carol F. Karlsen, *The Devil in the Shape of a Woman: Witchcraft in Colonial New England* (New York, 1987); Demos, *Entertaining Satan*; Stephen Boyer and John Nissenbaum, *Salem Possessed: The Social Origins of Witchcraft* (Cambridge, Mass., 1974); Chadwick Hansen, *Witchcraft at Salem* (New York, 1969); and Konig, *Law and Society*.

About lawyers in England, see generally Holdsworth, *History of English Law*, and E. W. Ives, *The Common Lawyers of Pre-Reformation England* (Cambridge, 1983). The student might also consult Brooks, *Pettifoggers and vipers of the Commonwealth*; Harry Kirk, *Portrait of a Profession* (London, 1976); Wilfred Prest, ed., *Lawyers in Early Modern Europe and America* (New York, 1981); and Robert Robson, *The Attorney in Eighteenth-Century England* (Cambridge, 1959).

Regulation of the colonial economies is traced in Richard B. Morris, *Government and Labor in Early America* (New York, 1947). Regulation in the cities is discussed in Gary B. Nash, *The Urban Crucible: Social Change, Political Consciousness, and the Origins of the American Revolution* (Cambridge, Mass.,

1979). On the regulation of the tobacco market, see T. H. Breen, *Tobacco Culture: The Mentality of the Great Tidewater Planters on the Eve of the Revolution* (Princeton, 1985).

Chapter Three

I have taken the case of Richard Wayte from James F. Cooper, "The Confession and Trial of Richard Wayte, Boston, 1640," *William and Mary Quarterly*, 3d ser., 44 (1987): 310–32. The figures on lawyers from Hampshire and Worcester Counties are from Gerald W. Gawalt, *The Promise of Power: The Emergence of the Legal Profession in Massachusetts, 1760–1840*, (Westport, Conn., 1979), 29, 42. The Massachusetts data is derived from David Thomas Konig, ed., *Plymouth County Court Records, 1686–1859* (Wilmington, Del., 1979), vols. 5, 10, and 13; Christine Heyrman, *Commerce and Culture: The Maritime Communities of Colonial Massachusetts, 1690–1750* (New York, 1984); Konig, *Law and Society*; William E. Nelson, *Dispute and Conflict Resolution in Plymouth County, Massachusetts, 1725–1825* (Chapel Hill, 1981); and Peter E. Russell, *His Majesty's Judges: Provincial Society and the Superior Court in Massachusetts, 1692–1774* (New York, 1990). On Connecticut, I have used Cornelia Hughes Dayton, "Women before the Bar: Gender, Law, and Society in Connecticut, 1710–1790" (Ph.D. diss., Princeton University, 1986), and Bruce Mann, *Neighbors and Strangers: Law and Community in Early Connecticut* (Chapel Hill, 1987). On the Delaware Valley, one can consult William McEnery Offutt, Jr., "Law and Social Cohesion in a Plural Society: The Delaware Valley, 1680–1710" (Ph.D. diss., The Johns Hopkins University, 1987).

My population figures are from Evarts B. Greene and Virginia D. Harrington, *American Population before the Federal Census of 1790* (New York, 1932), and I have assumed, following Robert V. Wells, *The Population of the British Colonies in America before 1776: A Survey of Census Data* (Princeton, 1975), 83, 85, 92, 93, that the sex ratio was about 1.07 males per female and that the adult population (over fifteen) was about 52 percent of the total population. I use adult population since minors were not allowed to bring lawsuits in their own behalf. The calculation of rates is my own and is very approximate. For a fuller version of the argument here, see Peter Charles Hoffer, "Honor and the Roots of American Litigiousness," *American Journal of Legal History* 33 (1989): 295–319.

For another view of law as a communal boundary maker, see Emile Durkheim's views on deviance in *The Rules of Sociological Method*, tr. S. A. Solvaay and G. H. Mueller (New York, 1958), 67. The analysis of the New York cases can be found in Rosen, "The Supreme Court of Judicature of Colonial New York," 239. I have taken the account of *Byfield v. Blagrove* from Barbara A. Black, "Nathaniel Byfield, 1653–1733" in Coquillette, ed., *Law in Colonial Massachusetts*, 57–106.

The general issue of wrangling between assemblies and governors is traced in Jack P. Greene, *The Quest for Power: The Lower Houses of Assembly in the*

Southern Royal Colonies, 1689–1776 (Chapel Hill, 1963); Sosin, *The Aristocracy of the Long Robe*, 139–86; and Bernard Bailyn, *The Origins of American Politics* (New York, 1968), 59–105. The particular course of this struggle for control of purse and power is found in every volume of the colonial history series edited by Milton Klein for K. T. O. Press. See, for example, on the Maryland and New York assemblies mentioned in the text, C. Aubrey Land, *Colonial Maryland—A History* (Millwood, N.Y., 1984), and Michael Kammen, *Colonial New York—A History* (New York, 1975). On the New Jersey assembly, see Thomas Purvis's excellent *Proprietors, Patronage, and Paper Money: Legislative Politics in New Jersey, 1703–1776* (New Brunswick, N.J., 1986).

Chapter Four

The periodization of law is always a speculative venture. As Stanley Katz long ago reminded us, any periodization of law, or rather, of legal change, tends to foreshorten the actual process by which the change took place. Common law changes very slowly; statute law looks faster, but it is often the product—the end product—of far more leisurely changes in legal practice. See Katz, "Looking Backward—The Early History of American Law," *University of Chicago Law Review* 33 (1966): 867–84. Despite these very wise warnings, I am convinced that the Glorious Revolution in England wrought visible and important changes in the structure and practice of law in the colonies.

The increased role of English lawyers in American law is supported by Joseph H. Smith, *Appeals to the Privy Council*, and in shortened form, Smith, "Administrative Control of the Courts," in Flaherty, ed., *Essays in the History of Early American Law*, 282–332. On the passage of English law treatises into the colonies, see William Hamilton Bryson, *Census of Law Books in Colonial Virginia* (Charlottesville, 1978), and Herbert A. Johnson, *Imported Eighteenth-Century Law Treatises in American Libraries, 1700–1799* (Knoxville, 1978).

On the rise of the American legal profession, see Stephen Botein, "The Legal Profession in Colonial North America," in Prest, ed., *Lawyers in Early Modern Europe and America*, 121–46; Gawalt, *The Promise of Power*; John M. Murrin, "The Legal Transformation: The Bench and Bar of Eighteenth-Century Massachusetts," in Stanley N. Katz, ed., *Colonial America: Essays in Politics and Social Development* (Boston, 1971), 415–49; A. G. Roeber, *Faithful Magistrates and Republican Lawyers: Creators of Virginia Legal Culture, 1680–1810* (Chapel Hill, 1981); Alan F. Day, *A Social Study of Lawyers in Maryland, 1660–1775* (New York, 1990); John T. Farrell, ed., *The Superior Court Diary of William Samuel Johnson, 1772–1773* (Washington, D.C., 1942); and Frank L. Dewey, *Thomas Jefferson—Lawyer* (Charlottesville, 1986).

On legal education, see Paul M. Hamlin, *Legal Education in Colonial New York* (New York, 1939), and the introductions to Julius Goebel, Jr., et al., eds., *The Law Practice of Alexander Hamilton: Documents and Commentary* (New York, 1964), 1:1–182; L. Kinvin Wroth and Hiller B. Zobel, eds., *The Legal Papers of John Adams* (Cambridge, Mass., 1965), 1: xxxi–xlvi, 1–25; and Her-

bert A. Johnson et al., eds., *The Papers of John Marshall* (Chapel Hill, 1974–),
1:37–86.

The role of the county court clerk is discussed in David Thomas Konig,
"Country Justice: The Rural Roots of Constitutionalism in Colonial Virginia,"
in Kermit L. Hall and James W. Ely, Jr., eds., *An Uncertain Tradition: Constitutionalism in the History of the South* (Athens, Ga., 1989), 63–82. Marmaduke Beckwith's impact upon law in Richmond County is traced in Peter
Charles Hoffer's "Introduction" to Hoffer and William B. Scott, eds., *Criminal
Proceedings in Colonial Virginia: The Richmond County Record . . . 1711–
1754* (Washington, D.C., and Athens, Ga., 1984), ix–xi.

The colonial version of the writ pleading system is discussed in Konig,
"Introduction," *Plymouth County Court Records*, 1:149–73; William E. Nelson, *Americanization of the Common Law: The Impact of Legal Change on
Massachusetts Society, 1760–1830* (Cambridge, Mass., 1975); and Stephan
Landesman, "The Rise of the Contentious Spirit: Adversary Procedure in Eighteenth-Century England," *Cornell Law Review* 75 (1990): 497–609. A general
introduction to the English system is Frederick G. Kempin, Jr., *Historical Introduction to Anglo-American Law in a Nutshell*, rev. ed. (St. Paul, 1973). For
greater detail, one should see Baker's *Introduction to English Legal History*.

The origins of the actions for land, torts, and promises appear in Plucknett's
Concise History and Baker's *Introduction to English Legal History*. On the
internal coherence of Blackstone's thought, see Daniel Boorstin, *The Mysterious Science of the Law: An Essay on Blackstone's Commentaries* (Boston,
1958), and Duncan Kennedy, "The Structure of Blackstone's Commentaries,"
Buffalo Law Review 28 (1979): 205 and after, but see Alan Watson, "The Structure of Blackstone's Commentaries," *Yale Law Journal* 97 (1988): 795 and after
for a rebuttal of Kennedy.

On land law in the colonies, see Morris, *Studies in the History of American
Law*, 69–125. Beverley W. Bond, Jr., *The Quit-Rent System in the American
Colonies* (New Haven, 1919), is still a good source on the rents charged by king
and proprietor and hardly ever paid by colonial occupiers of land.

The scholarly literature on inheritance, along with a massive empirical
study of actual descent of property, is cataloged in Carol Shammas, Marylynn
Salmon, and Michel Dahlin, *Inheritance in America, from Colonial Times to
the Present* (New Brunswick, N.J., 1987). Kenneth Lockridge, *Literacy in Colonial New England* (New York, 1974), uses signatures to wills as a measure of
literacy. I have taken the account of the German migrants' response to English
inheritance laws from A. G. Roeber, "'We Hold These Truths . . .' : German
and Anglo-American Concepts of Property and Inheritance in the Eighteenth
Century" (Paper read to the Philadelphia Center for Early American Studies,
November 1989).

On women and the law of property, one should see Salmon, *Women and the
Law of Property in Early America* (Chapel Hill, 1986), and Joan R. Gunderson
and Gwen Victor Gampel, "Married Women's Legal Status in Eighteenth-Century New York and Virginia," *William and Mary Quarterly*, 3d ser., 39 (1982):
114–34. A comparison of English and American treatment of women in the

seventeenth century is Roger Thompson, *Women in Stuart England and America* (London, 1974). On married women's property and the law in England during this period, see Susan Staves, *Married Women's Separate Property in England, 1660–1833* (Cambridge, Mass., 1990).

Divorce law is explored in Roderick Phillips, *Putting Asunder: A History of Divorce in Western Society* (Cambridge, 1988): Nancy F. Cott, "Divorce and the Changing Status of Women in Eighteenth-Century Massachusetts," *William and Mary Quarterly*, 3d ser., 33 (1976): 586–615; and Dayton, "Women before the Bar."

On the churches and church law, see Carl Bridenbaugh, *Mitre and Sceptre: Transatlantic Faiths, Ideas, Personalities, and Politics, 1689–1775* (New York, 1962); Isaac, *The Transformation of Virginia*; Frederick B. Tolles, *Meeting House and Counting House: The Quaker Merchants of Colonial Philadelphia, 1682–1763* (Chapel Hill, 1948); Nelson, *Dispute and Conflict Resolution*; and Emil Oberholtzer, Jr., *Delinquent Saints: Disciplinary Action in the Early Congregational Churches of Massachusetts* (New York, 1956). The effects of the great awakening are traced in C. C. Goen, *Revivalism and Separatism in New England, 1740–1800* (New Haven, 1962); Alan Heimert, *Religion and the American Mind, from the Great Awakening to the Revolution* (Cambridge, Mass., 1966); Heimert and Perry Miller, eds., *The Great Awakening* (Indianapolis, 1967); Henry F. May, *The Enlightenment in America* (New York, 1976); and Gregory H. Nobles, *Divisions throughout the Whole: Politics and Society in Hampshire County, Massachusetts, 1740–1775* (Cambridge, 1983).

On crime in eighteenth-century England see J. M. Beattie, *Crime and the Courts in England, 1660–1800* (Princeton, 1986); Cockburn, *Assizes*, and Cockburn, ed., *Crime in England, 1550–1800* (London, 1977); Hay et al., *Albion's Fatal Tree*; Thompson, *Whigs and Hunters*; and John H. Langbein, "The Criminal Trial before the Lawyers," *University of Chicago Law Review* 45 (1978): 263–316

On court and crime in later seventeenth-century New England, one should see Oberholtzer, *Delinquent Saints*; N. E. H. Hull, *Female Felons: Women and Serious Crime in Colonial Massachusetts* (Urbana, Ill., 1987); Haskins, *Law and Authority*; and David S. Flaherty, "Crime and Social Control in Provincial Massachusetts," *Historical Journal* 24 (1981). Crime and social control in Virginia are discussed in Hoffer, "Introduction," in Hoffer and Scott, eds., *Criminal Proceedings*; Hugh F. Rankin, *Criminal Trial Proceedings in the General Court of Colonial Virginia* (Williamsburg, 1965); and Arthur P. Scott, *Criminal Law in Colonial Virginia* (Chicago, 1930).

On crime and justice in New York, see Julius N. Goebel, Jr., and T. Raymond Naughton, *Law Enforcement in Colonial New York: A Study in Criminal Procedure, 1664–1776* (New York, 1944), and Douglas Greenberg, *Crime and Law Enforcement in the Colony of New York, 1692–1776* (Ithaca, N.Y., 1976). On the Carolinas, see Donna Spindel, *Crime and Society in North Carolina, 1673–1776* (Baton Rouge, 1989), and Michael Stephen Hindus, *Prison and Plantation: Crime, Justice, and Authority in Massachusetts and South Carolina, 1767–1878* (Chapel Hill, 1980).

On the criminal jury in England and America, see J. S. Cockburn and Thomas A. Green, eds., *Twelve Good Men and True: The Jury in Early Modern England* (Princeton, 1988); Green, *Verdict according to Conscience: Perspectives on the English Criminal Trial Jury, 1200–1800* (Chicago, 1985); and John M. Murrin, "Magistrates, Sinners, and a Precarious Liberty: Trial by Jury in Seventeenth-Century New England," in Hall et al., eds., *Saints and Revolutionaries*, 152–206.

On the Zenger trial as an episode in the history of free press, see Leonard W. Levy, *The Emergence of a Free Press* (New York, 1985), and Stephen Botein, "The Trial of John Peter Zenger: Transatlantic Perspectives" (Paper presented at the 1985 Conference on Legal History in Early America, New-York Historical Society, May 1987). The Zenger trial has also been regarded as a milestone in our political history; see Stanley N. Katz, "Introduction," in Katz, ed., *A Brief Narrative of the Case and Trial of John Peter Zenger*, by James Alexander (Cambridge, Mass., 1963), 1–35; Paul Finkelman, "The Zenger Case: Prototype of a Political Trial," in Michal R. Belknap, ed., *American Political Trials* (Westport, Conn., 1981), 21–42; and Richard B. Morris, "The Zenger Trial," in Morris, *Fair Trial* (New York, 1952), 69–95. David H. Flaherty assessed the impact of criminal lawyers on the outcomes of trials in "Criminal Practice in Provincial Massachusetts," in Coquillette, ed., *Law in Colonial Massachusetts*, 191–242.

On the grand juries, one should see Gwenda Morgan, *The Hegemony of the Law, Richmond County, Virginia, 1692–1776* (New York, 1989); Dayton, "Women before the Bar"; Offutt, "Law and Social Cohesion"; as well as the books on crime listed above. The rising tide of premarital pregnancy is documented in Edward Shorter, *The Making of the Modern Family*, 2d ed. (New York, 1977), and Daniel Scott Smith and Michael Hindus, "Premarital Pregnancy in America, 1640–1971: An Overview and Interpretation," *Journal of Interdisciplinary History* 5 (1975): 537–70.

The literature on slavery and the law in early America is voluminous, and there is no way to do it justice here. In addition to the works cited in the text, one ought to consult David Brion Davis, *The Problem of Slavery in the Age of Revolution, 1770–1823* (Ithaca, N.Y., 1975); Alan Watson, *Slave Law in the Americas* (Athens, Ga., 1989); William Wiecek, *The Sources of Antislavery Constitutionalism in America* (Ithaca, N.Y., 1977); and Arthur Zilversmit, *The First Emancipation: The Abolition of Slavery in the North* (Chicago, 1967). On the racial basis of slavery, see Winthrop Jordan, *White over Black* (Chapel Hill, 1968), and Orlando Patterson's *Slavery and Social Death: A Comparative Study* (Cambridge, Mass., 1982).

The idea that slaves contributed to the criminal law is a central theme in Philip J. Schwarz, *Twice Condemned: Slaves and the Criminal Laws of Virginia, 1705–1865* (Baton Rouge, 1988). On convict laborers as an alternative labor force, see A. Roger Ekirch, *Bound for America: The Transportation of British Convicts to the Colonies, 1718–1775* (Oxford, 1987). Peter H. Wood, *Black Majority: Negroes in Colonial South Carolina from 1670 through the*

Stono Rebellion (New York, 1974), reminds readers of how much more than mere labor the Africans brought to the colonies.

The notion of "bi-formities" in law is explored in Michael Kammen, *People of Paradox: An Inquiry concerning the Origins of American Civilization* (New York, 1972), 89–116.

Chapter Five

Good general sources on the intellectual concussions of the civil-war era in England are John W. Gough, *Fundamental Law in English Constitutional History* (Oxford, 1961); Christopher Hill, *Intellectual Origins of the English Revolution* (Oxford, 1965) and *The World Turned Upside Down* (London, 1972); J. G. A. Pocock, *The Ancient Constitution and the Feudal Law* (Cambridge, 1957); Quentin Skinner, *The Foundations of Modern Political Thought, Vol. 2, The Age of Reformation* (Cambridge, 1978); and Richard Tuck, *Natural Rights Theories: Their Origin and Development* (Cambridge, 1979). Two essential constitutional documentary collections are J. P. Kenyon's *Stuart Constitution* (Cambridge, 1966) and E. N. Williams, ed., *The Eighteenth-Century Constitution* (Cambridge, 1960).

Accounts of the English Civil War, the Protectorate, the Restoration, and the Glorious Revolution of 1689, were they weeds, would choke this bibliography. There are excellent bibliographies in J. R. Jones, *Country and Court: England, 1658–1714* (Cambridge, Mass., 1979); at the end of the essays in E. W. Ives, ed., *The English Revolution, 1600–1660* (New York, 1971); and in Donald Pennington and Keith Thomas, eds., *Puritans and Revolutionaries* (Oxford, 1978).

C. B. MacPherson's *Political Theory of Possessive Individualism* (Oxford, 1962) set off a furious debate on the meaning and intent of Locke's work. One should see Peter Laslett's edition of Locke's *Two Treatises*, rev. ed. (Cambridge, 1967), for a superb edition of the text; Caroline Robbins' *Absolute Liberty*, ed. Barbara Taft (Hamden, Conn., 1982); John W. Yolton, ed., *John Locke: Problems and Perspectives* (Cambridge, 1969); and Howard Nenner, *By Color of Law: Legal Culture and Constitutional Politics in England, 1600–1689* (Chicago, 1977). Harrington's *Oceana*, with commentary, can be found in J. G. A. Pocock, ed., *The Political Writings of James Harrington* (Cambridge, 1977).

On the commonwealthmen, see Caroline Robbins, *The Eighteenth-Century Commonwealthman* (Cambridge, Mass., 1959), and J. R. Pole, *Political Representation in England and the Origins of the American Republic* (Berkeley, 1966). The "idea" of civic humanism is fully described in J. G. A. Pocock, *The Machiavellian Moment: Florentine Political Thought and the Atlantic Republican Tradition* (Princeton, 1975). On John Adams' application of these ideas to the American Revolution, see John R. Howe, Jr., *The Changing Political Ideas of John Adams* (Princeton, 1966), and Gordon Wood, *The Creation of the American Republic, 1776–1787* (Chapel Hill, 1969). A psychological approach is essayed in Peter Shaw, *The Character of John Adams* (Chapel Hill, 1975).

The notion of an American common law arising out of the briefs of the revolutionary lawyers is hinted at in John P. Reid, *Briefs of the American Revolution* (New York, 1981). The "memory exercise" of American judicial rule making is Julius Goebel's remark; see *Law Practice of Alexander Hamilton*, 1:43.

On the Parson's Cause and the Writs of Assistance, see Bernard Bailyn, *The Ordeal of Thomas Hutchinson* (Cambridge, 1974); Lawrence H. Gipson, *The Coming of the Revolution, 1763–1775* (New York, 1954); Maurice H. Smith, *The Writs of Assistance Case* (Berkeley, 1978); John J. Waters, Jr., *The Otis Family in Provincial and Revolutionary Massachusetts* (Chapel Hill, 1968); and William Cuddihy and B. Carmon Hardy, "A Man's House Was Not His Castle: Origins of the Fourth Amendment to the United States Constitution," *William and Mary Quarterly*, 3d ser., 37 (1980): 371–400. The McDougall case is traced in Roger J. Champagne, *Alexander McDougall and the American Revolution in New York* (Schenectady, N.Y., 1975), and Leslie F. Upton, *The Loyal Whig: William Smith of New York and Quebec* (Toronto, 1969). The Boston Massacre and the trials of Captain Preston and his men are narrated in Hiller B. Zobel, *The Boston Massacre* (New York, 1970). I have taken the text of Quincy and Adams' defense of the soldiers from *The Trial of the British Soldiers . . .* (Boston, 1807). The Wilkesites' use of trials to make political speeches is explained in John Brewer, "The Wilkesites and the Law, 1763–1764: A Study of Radical Notions of Governance," in Brewer and Styles, eds., *An Ungovernable People*, 131–56.

The debate over the influence of common law on the revolutionaries' arguments pits John Reid, *The Constitutional History of the American Revolution, Vol. 1, The Authority of Rights* (Madison, 1986–89), and *Vol. 2: The Authority to Tax* (Madison, 1987), 276–77: "Part and parcel of the constitutional heritage that the colonists shared with the British was a common constitutional language. Constitutional principles were expressed in formulas that belonged to a taught legal tradition, using language that could have originated on either side of the Atlantic," against Bernard Bailyn, *The Ideological Origins of the American Revolution* (Cambridge, Mass., 1967), 31: "the common law was manifestly influential in shaping the awareness of the revolutionary generation. But, again, it did not in itself determine the kinds of conclusions men would draw in the crisis of the time. . . . The law was no science of what to do next." Reid says the issue is a quarrel over the constitution, and his examples are drawn from supposedly fundamental, shared notions of "property" and "rights." In a sense he has returned us to the argument of Charles McIlwain and other early twentieth-century scholars. Reid concedes that politics played a part in this discourse over constitutional rights, but the legal discourse is the central part of his story. Bailyn is also vitally concerned with ideas, but they are the political ideas of the commonwealthmen and their intellectual debtors on the American shore. He believes that Real Whigs, not the lawyers, gave intellectual coherence, as well as urgency, to the revolutionary movement.

There are other parties in this dispute. Barbara Black, "The Constitution of Empire: The Case for the Colonists," *University of Pennsylvania Law Review*

124 (1976): 1157–1211, and Jack P. Greene, *Peripheries and Center: Constitutional Development in the Extended Polities of the British Empire and the United States, 1607–1788* (Athens, Ga., 1986), have joined Reid in his siege of Bailyn's position. The reference to "arbitrary power" comes from Reid, *The Concept of Liberty in the Age of the American Revolution* (Chicago, 1988), 106.

On the Oliver impeachment, see Peter Charles Hoffer and N. E. H. Hull, *Impeachment in America, 1635–1805* (New Haven, 1984). The course of the Continental Congress is most recently traced in Jerrilyn Greene Marston, *King and Congress: The Transfer of Political Legitimacy, 1774–1776* (Princeton, 1987), and Jack N. Rakove, *The Beginnings of National Politics: An Interpretive History of the Continental Congress* (New York, 1979).

The first state constitutions are discussed in a wide variety of works, some by political scientists and lawyers, others by historians. Old standards include Elisha P. Douglass, *Rebels and Democrats: The Struggle for Equal Political Rights and Majority Rule during the American Revolution* (Chapel Hill, 1955); Merrill Jensen, *The Articles of Confederation* (Madison, 1948); and Allan R. Nevins, *The American States during and after the Revolution, 1775–1789* (New York, 1924). The greatest of the modern classics is Gordon Wood, *The Creation of the American Republic, 1776–1787* (Chapel Hill, 1969). One of the most suggestive of recent studies is Donald S. Lutz, *Popular Consent and Popular Control: Whig Political Theory in the Early State Constitutions* (Baton Rouge, 1980).

On the authority of the assembly, I have relied on Greene, *The Quest for Power*; Lawrence Leder, *Liberty and Authority: Early American Political Ideology, 1689–1763* (Chicago, 1968), and Bailyn, *The Origins of American Politics*. These authors do not quite agree on the role of the assembly, and the best way to resolve their differences is to examine each colony separately.

Party formation in these first new governments is traced in Jackson Turner Main, *Political Parties before Constitution* (Chapel Hill, 1973), and Pauline Maier, *The Old Revolutionaries: Political Lives in the Age of Samuel Adams* (New York, 1980), as well as the works of Nevins and Jensen. On the profiteering of the staff officers, see E. Wayne Carp, *To Starve the Army at Pleasure: Continental Army Administration and American Political Culture, 1775–1783* (Chapel Hill, 1984), and Charles Royster, *A Revolutionary People at War: The Continental Army and American Character, 1775–1783* (Chapel Hill, 1979).

The changing nature of "property" and "liberty" is, as I write, a hotly contested issue. One may see the exchange between Lance Banning and Joyce Appleby in *William and Mary Quarterly*, 3d ser., 43 (1986): 3–34. Appleby's *Capitalism and a New Social Order: The Republican Vision of the 1790s* (New York, 1984) is in part a response to Banning's own *Jeffersonian Persuasion: Evolution of a Party Ideology* (Ithaca, N.Y., 1978) and Drew R. McCoy's *Elusive Republic: Political Economy in Jeffersonian America* (Chapel Hill, 1980), and in part an extension of her own *Economic Thought and Ideology in Seventeenth-Century England* (Princeton, 1978). The student might also consult Michael Kammen, *Spheres of Liberty: Changing Perceptions of Liberty in American Culture* (Madison, 1986). Revolutionary ideas of property are the subject of the essays in Ellen Frankel Paul and Howard Dickman, eds., *Liberty, Property, and the Foundations of the American Constitution* (Albany, 1989).

Conclusion

On king and people, see Richard Bushman, *King and People in Provincial Massachusetts* (Chapel Hill, 1985). For a definition of law as the will of the state ratified by the consent of the people, see H. L. A. Hart, *The Concept of Law* (Oxford, 1961), 97.

My discussion of Rule of Law derives from a wonderful seminar under that title taught at Harvard Law School over the course of the 1986–87 year by Professor William Fisher III. Students interested in the concept of Rule of Law might want to pursue the subject in Lon L. Fuller, *The Morality of Law*, 2d ed. (New Haven, 1969), and Theodore Lowi, *The End of Liberalism*, rev. ed. (New York, 1969). Modified versions of Rule of Law appear in Marver Bernstein, *Regulating Business by Independent Commission* (Princeton, 1955), and Jerry L. Mashaw, *Due Process in the Administrative State* (New Haven, 1985).

INDEX

Abolitionism, of slavery in American colonies, 94
Accountability of government, 99
Actions. See Writs
Act to Prevent Fraud of 1660, 103
Adams, John: on legal education, 65, 112–13; on juries, 88; as revolutionary advocate, 101; and Boston Massacre, 106–7; "Thoughts on Government," 114; and Rule of Law, 122–23
Adams, Samuel, and Boston Massacre, 106
Admiralty Act of 1696, 103
Adultery, 19
Africans, brought to America, 90
Allen, David Grayson, on origins of colonial law, 135–36
"American common law," 100, 109
"Anglicization" of American law, 66, 94, 107
Apostasy, 19
Appeal, 26, 35–37
Appleby, Joyce, on self-interest, 120
Arbitration, 31, 48, 49
Arson, 92–93
Assault, 7, 83
Attorneys, 41, 64
Avery, Waitstill, on criminal law practice, 87

Bacon, Francis, 5
Bailyn, Bernard: on migration to New World, 1; on revolutionary ideology, 99, 148; on "contagion of liberty," 115
Baker, John, on Edward Coke, 4
Baptists, 80
Bar associations, 66
Barbados, slave law in, 90
Barristers, 41
Bastardy, 83, 89
Battery, 7, 83

Beckwith, Marmaduke, and local courts, 67
Benefit of clergy, 81
Benson, Egbert, 113
Bestiality, 82
Beverley, Robert, on law in Virginia, 33, 45
Bible, 17, 19, 81
Bills of attainder, 117
Bills of rights, 31, 84, 114
Black, Barbara, on Nathaniel Byfield, 57
Blackstone, William, on liberty, 98
Blagrove, Nathaniel, 57–58
Blasphemy, 19
Bonds, to keep the peace, 7, 84
Book debt, 53
Book law, x, xi, 2, 3, 4–5
Books of orders, 8, 9
Boston, Massachusetts: standard of living in, 62; slavery in, 92; "Massacre" of 1770, 105–7; "Tea Party," 112; in wartime, 112
Bristol County, Massachusetts, 57
Brown, Purchase, inheritance of, 71
Buggery, 82
Bureaucracy, and law enforcement, 97
Burglary, 82
Bushman, Richard, on king and law, 122
Byfield, Nathaniel, 57–58

Capitalism, 10
Capital offenses, 81
Carolinas, 10, 70
Catholicism, 76, 78, 93
Chancellors. See Equity
Charles I, 12, 22
Charles II, 32, 45
Charters for American colonies, ix, 2, 11–14
Chattels, 71, 72–73
Chesapeake, 1, 22

Designed by Laury A. Egan

Composed by G & S Typesetters, Inc.,
in Pilgrim text and display.

Printed on 55-lb. Sebago Antique Cream
and bound in Joanna Arrestox cloth
by The Maple Press Company.